BY GENEEN ROTH

This Messy Magnificent Life: A Field Guide

Women Food and God

Lost and Found

When Food Is Love

The Craggy Hole in My Heart and the Cat Who Fixed It

Breaking Free from Emotional Eating

Feeding the Hungry Heart

When You Eat at the Refrigerator, Pull Up a Chair

Appetites: On the Search for True Nourishment

Why Weight? A Guide to Ending Compulsive Eating

LOVE, FINALLY

LOVE, FINALLY

Untangling the Knot Between Mothers, Daughters, and Food

GENEEN ROTH

Foreword by Anne Lamott

THE DIAL PRESS

New York

The Dial Press
An imprint of Random House
A division of Penguin Random House LLC
1745 Broadway, New York, NY 10019
randomhousebooks.com
penguinrandomhouse.com

Hardcover ISBN 978-0-593-73373-8
Ebook ISBN 978-0-593-73374-5
Printed in the United States of America

1st Printing

First Edition

Book Team: Production editor: Andy Lefkowitz • Managing editor: Rebecca Berlant • Production manager: Sandra Sjursen • Copy editor: Jennifer Prior • Proofreaders: Dan Goff, Marcell Rosenblatt, and Barbara Stussy

Book design by Debbie Glasserman

The authorized representative in the EU for product safety and compliance is Penguin Random House Ireland, Morrison Chambers, 32 Nassau Street, Dublin D02 YH68, Ireland.
https://eu-contact.penguin.ie

For my mother

and

For Coco and the girls

"We don't see things as they are, we see them as we are."

ANAÏS NIN

"The world is made of rings. The hooks are yours. Make straight your hooks and nothing can hold you."

SRI NISARGADATTA MAHARAJ

"There are no facts, only interpretations."

FRIEDRICH NIETZSCHE

CONTENTS

FOREWORD

This is a culmination of Geneen Roth's work of the past forty years, of what it takes to emerge from obsession and self-rejection. And it is an uncommon love story between a mother and daughter, between a woman and her past, between a precious body and itself.

I loved traveling with Geneen through the brambles and swamps, meadows and thickets and glades, as she unspooled new truth about food, mothers, and self-rejection, and in the process discovered "who you are when you aren't your wounds." You're perfect, is her message, a gorgeous wild soul with skin on.

There are so many lines that I could quote here, which I first underlined and then copied onto Post-it notes that I stuck on the wall. One in particular made me laugh out loud. "Variety is not my friend." No one in my seven decades here has ever before captured why I love and eat from a rather limited repertoire. Variety and too many choices are absolutely not my friends. If I stick to a simple plan of proteins, lots of greens, fruit, and grains, and stay away from sugar and white flour, the pond inside of me stays settled. I don't need to try a lot of new things—ancient oils, unborn baby lettuce, eggplant icicle—I do not need a white eggplant! The very words make me nervous.

Go ahead. You eat the damn eggplant icicle. I'm sticking to the purple and the black. Geneen has helped me learn to ask for what I need and want, and that "No" is a complete sentence, and to feel safe again around food and my body. When she writes about the often unconscious and heartbreaking unkindness she has turned on herself, I nod, groaning, and when she offers a remarkably simple way of undoing a lifetime of pain, of finding respite, I rejoice.

I don't know how she does it again and again, creating prose and stories that move from the universal to the specifics of a rather harrowing binge, from the spiritually uplifting to the outrageously funny. As someone said about her, she puts into words what we know that we don't know we know.

And she's done it again, thrown the lights on for us in her inimitable and compelling way, in this *most* important book so far. Listen: "The distance between being happy and being miserable is made of the lies we tell ourselves. And the way to see through our mind-made conclusions is to name and question them, beginning with the awareness that we are making them up. This is what it means to come home to ourselves, to the sweetness of love itself." Love its very own pure self, finally.

I invite you to come on in.

—ANNE LAMOTT

LOVE, FINALLY

PROLOGUE:
TAPIOCA PUDDING

My mother and I are in the kitchen unloading bags of groceries from Key Food. First the tub of cottage cheese, then the package of Velveeta. I grab the dark blue-and-white Horn & Hardart container of tapioca pudding and it slips out of my hand, spills onto the floor. I am twelve years old.

Uh-oh, I think. *I'm in trouble.* But my mother bursts into laughter. "Look at all those squishy tapioca balls," she says, bending down. "Let's play with them. Come, sit on the floor."

"Play with balls of tapioca? With you?"

"Yes," she says. "Let's do it before we clean it up."

We sit on the floor and spread out the pudding like paint. Then we smear our hands in glops of it, squish the balls between our fingers, laugh at how slimy it feels.

"It's okay to play with food every once in a while," my mother says. "To take a break from counting calories and mush your hands in it."

Sixty years later I remember the slant of pale January light on her shiny penny loafer. Her fingers covered in pudding. My astonishment at being given permission to be naughty, at laughing instead of crying about food. At having a mother who seemed to love me. I keep this memory like a tiny emerald in my back pocket. For years, I believed that the tapioca mother was my real mother and that she would become her again if I could just hold out long enough. Eventually I understood that it was me whom I'd waited half a century to meet again.

INTRODUCTION

As far back as I can remember, when I didn't feel love, I ate. Food was my secret way of giving to myself. It was also a way to hurt myself. I inhaled. I hid. I stole. Which proved that I was bad, damaged, doomed.

At eleven, sixteen, twenty-five, I punished myself with food the way my mother punished me with her hands. In the middle of twenty-thousand-calorie binges, insane with self-hatred, I'd chant: *Good. Again. Harder.* Until, when I was twenty-seven, having gained and lost more than a thousand pounds—the equivalent of a horse or a baby grand piano—in seventeen years, I decided I had two choices: kill myself or stop dieting. I could not recall a single minute of my life until that point when I had been diet- or binge-free.

I stopped dieting.

Within two days, I felt exuberant, giddy, released.

Within a week, I knew I'd discovered a way out of hell.

Within a month, I started a dollar-a-night group for eight women to examine the ways we punished ourselves with food.

Within two months, I'd lost ten pounds by eating when I was hungry and stopping when I was full. I knew then that if I, who was as insane as anyone I'd ever met about food and weight, could break free from compulsive eating, anyone could—and I wanted to shout that discovery to women everywhere, so I did the next best thing: I wrote a book about it. Then ten more.

For the next forty years, I led workshops and retreats for thousands of women about using their relationship with food to change how they lived. One of those books, *Women Food and God,* became a number one *New York Times* bestseller. I spoke in stadiums, lecture halls, universities, appeared on *Oprah.* And yet. I woke up day after day haunted by a feeling that something was wrong and I was to blame. Years of spiritual practice and decades of good therapy softened but did not disappear the underlying discontent and self-hatred. Although compulsive eating had ceased to be an issue, I still believed that true happiness was possible for other people, just not me. The fact that I had a successful career, close friends, and was married to a man I loved, seemed like it should transform my chronic sense of being irrevocably damaged—only it didn't, even though I got pretty damn good at acting as if I were normal, sane, whole.

Sound crazy?

Nah.

As I've discovered, I'm not alone. Most of us live with secret fears of being unworthy or unlovable playing in the background like a scratchy soundtrack. We may conceal our underlying self-doubt and feelings of inadequacy with a topcoat of getting, having, working, trolling for likes on social media—the hallmarks of a "normal" life. Yet all the while our shame, anxiety, and negative self-judgment lie in wait, cruel masters that began with our earliest caregivers and have been shaping how we feel about ourselves, our relationships, and life itself ever since.

"Her pain became my element, the country in which I lived, the rule beneath which I bowed," wrote Vivian Gornick about her mother in her book *Fierce Attachments*. My mother's pain in her marriage to my father, her relationship with her own mother (by whom she felt hated), and her incessant negative judgments about her hair, her thighs, my hair, and my thighs were the air I breathed, the country in which I lived.

I cannot remember feeling loved or wanted by my mother.

Or a time when I was not aware of her loneliness.

Or a time that I didn't blame myself for being the kind of girl she couldn't love.

Even when she was hitting me, I apologized for being the kind of girl who deserved to get hit.

For the first twenty years of my thirty-nine-year marriage to Matt, a man I love madly, I continued to feel that I was unworthy of love—an underlying belief that neither a happy marriage nor worldly success could touch.

And so I jumped through every New Age, psychotherapeutic, and metaphysical hoop imaginable. I sat at the feet of gurus and enlightened masters, sampling the smorgasbord of spiritual teachings the way other people fill their plates at an all-you-can-eat buffet.

Yet, after all this, I was still just *me*.

Still convinced I was not the right person to be living my life.

I may have resolved my compulsive eating, but the deeper hunger to fix myself still plagued me. I abandoned my search for the one great teaching or teacher who could finally free me from the prison of my own self-hatred. Surprisingly, giving up was a relief. I didn't have to try—and fail—anymore. My life was good, even if inside I still felt broken.

Six years ago my friend Lizzy told me about a teacher named Coco—a seemingly ordinary, mostly blind eighty-year-old woman who spoke about the importance of "naming and dissolving unavoidable yet false conclusions" and "the awake awareness" that was revealed when those conclusions fell away—and I burst out laughing.

Seriously, another teacher?

Little did I know that when I decided to humor Lizzy and check out Coco's teachings, my lifelong wound would meet its medicine.

When I listened to Coco, I soon saw that the unease and discontent I often woke up with were based on conclusions I never remembered making—I'm damaged, I never get it right, I'm not enough—and that these conclusions could be questioned and eventually dissolved. When, on any old morning, I became aware of believing that I was damaged, I saw myself as a four-year-old, standing in front of my red-faced, screaming mother. I saw the confusion, the hurt, and the fear and I realized that her reaction was about her, not me. The infinite kindness I immediately felt for that four-year-old softened and began dissolving the conclusion. Eventually, after many times of noticing when I was triggered and realizing it was about a mistaken interpretation I'd made decades ago, the self-hatred began to dissipate; I stopped repeatedly and automatically rejecting myself. The conclusions became lighter, transparent, dissolved, until I understood that they were never true. I understood that it was possible for all of us—even the most hardcore self-doubters—to come home to ourselves and to the blooming galaxy of aliveness that is our birthright.

Even mine.

Here is what I know now: Losing weight is not the answer to anything but losing weight. Dropped pounds couldn't erase the buried shame and lies I believed about myself. While it's true that junky food leads to junky thoughts and that what we put into our mouths really does matter, it is also true that junky thoughts proliferate regardless of the food we eat. Sooner or later, usually sooner, our core beliefs about ourselves, our own worth, take center stage and run the show. Even when we are taking Ozempic or GLP-1 derivatives and the food noise is silenced. Even when we drop three jean sizes. Or when, as some women report, their moods are lifted and their shame about their bodies is eliminated. Even then we are still left with the predicament of seeing the world through the unavoidable conclusions we (unknowingly) made before we were seven years old. And of being swept into the cultural hypnosis of believing we are what we weigh.

After investigating my unavoidable and mistaken conclusions, I am not exaggerating when I say that although I look the same as I did before I met Coco (well, not exactly: more wrinkles, more cellulite, less hair), and my relationship with food is and will always be quirky (variety is not my friend), there is a lightness I've discovered, an openness that feels more like me than the me I thought was me.

Love, Finally is about giving ourselves permission to question what we've never questioned: that we see the world through our wounds, not as it really is. We see what we believe. And if we never question our conclusions about being unlovable or defective, those are the lenses through which we filter our experience. It's like seeing the entire world drenched in yellow when we're wearing yellow-tinted glasses. Freedom comes when we take the glasses off.

And, in a biblical event akin to the parting of the Red Sea, my turbulent relationship with my mother has become calm, peaceful, tender. As my self-loathing began to dissolve, my conversations with my mother lost their edges, became softer, rounder. I stopped being resentful about what she never was able to give me and began realizing what I already had. And what I can give myself. Miraculously, when I changed, so did she.

Still, we're human, and our deepening relationships with ourselves and one another are works in progress. Negative conclusions still arise, but now I catch them sooner than before and see them for what they really are: untrue. Then, with a newfound sense of freedom, I let them go.

The one thing I know for sure is that if I, this Eeyore-self, this daughter of an apparently angry, abusive, unhappy mother, can free herself from her sticky allegiance to old, hurtful stories, anyone can. Anyone can revel in the joy, magic, and peace that's been there all along.

And find love, finally.

PART ONE

Snookered

CHAPTER ONE

Sugar Smacks

It is June and time for my dreaded yearly physical. I am twelve years old. My mother walks with me to Dr. Modlin's office on the corner of our block. We pass our next-door neighbor Lucy Klein standing outside in her bright yellow muumuu hoisting up an American flag. We nod hello as my mother quietly whispers, "Someone needs to tell her that lipstick is supposed to stay on her lips and not touch her nose or her chin." We continue past Ethel and Fred Shapiro's house with the window box of bright red geraniums in front and past Marion and Len Singer's house with a rusted fountain in the yard.

Later, much later, my mother will call Dr. Modlin "a pig and a sadistic bastard" because he forgot to tell her that going cold turkey off the barbiturates he'd prescribed might kill her, which it almost did. But then, we lived on Eightieth Street in Jackson Heights, New York, and everyone on the block revered him because when you are Jewish, as we all were, a doctor is a step away from God.

I am frightened of Dr. Modlin. His wavy hair, his baritone voice, his rainfall of judgments about how fat I am. Every time I see him, which is weekly because he is my father's tennis partner and best friend, he tells me I am fat. He asks when I am going to lose weight.

As we get closer to his office, which is at the bottom level of his house, I look at the tiny stained-glass window of a swan in the corner and try to calm myself down because with each step, I feel more and more agitated. I tell my mother I feel sick. She says I am imagining it. I tell her I don't want to go into his office. She tells me I must go, that if I want to go to sleepaway camp, I must get a physical.

As soon as we ring the bell to his office, I throw up Sugar Smacks on his doorstep. My mother says, "Well, I guess you really were feeling sick."

Pat, the doctor's daughter, the one who told me she knew my mother before I did because she is four months older than I am, swings the carved wooden door open, notices the pool of half-digested cereal, and says, "Yuck." My mother says, "Pat, please tell your mother that Genie was sick outside the front door."

Inside Dr. Modlin's cave of an office I shiver and my hands shake. I step on the scale. Eighty-eight pounds. Dr. Modlin clucks his tongue. "You've gained twenty-two pounds since last year; you are getting fatter and fatter. You need to lose weight now." I turn to look at my mother, who is nodding. She thinks I am fat, too. The doctor listens to my breathing, thumps here and there for a few minutes, and tells me he is finished. As we are leaving, he says, "And you are allergic to chocolate, so if you are eating it, stop."

On our way home, my mother says, "Well, that wasn't so bad. It will be good for you to lose weight. And knowing that you are allergic to chocolate is also good."

"But how does he know I am allergic to chocolate?"

"Doctors know things that we don't," she says.

That night, I eat five frozen Milky Ways.

My mother is standing next to me as I reach into the refrigerator and pull out Dannon vanilla yogurt. She says, "Yogurt is fattening, too." I am fourteen and have been on a diet (or a binge) every day for three years.

I say, "What am I supposed to eat?"

She says, "As little as possible."

The next day I eat only Grape Nuts for breakfast, lunch, and dinner. She doesn't realize this because she is sleeping when I leave for school in the morning and out with her friends when I return. She doesn't like to cook. She isn't interested in what we eat or when, only the effect of it on my belly, arms, thighs.

When she took a baking class with her friend Mimi and brought home a warm cinnamon Bundt cake, my brother and I ate half of it immediately.

"That's the last time I ever bake anything," she said, furious. "It took hours to make it and it took you two minutes to eat. And besides, young lady," she says, glowering at me. "A minute on the lips is years on the hips, don't you know that by now?"

A month of eating only two apples a day follows the month of eating nothing but Grape Nuts. I don't think about nutrition. I don't think about protein. I think only about calories and limiting what I eat to less than a thousand calories a day. Still, I gain weight. My body, a boy in my class says, is made of circles.

When I get off the bus from camp at the end of the summer, my mother looks at me and says, "You are so fat you could have rolled off that bus." We go immediately to Dr. Mende, whose nurse, Cathy, sits in front of a desk with fifteen bins of colored capsules.

Cathy has platinum frosted hair, wears bright blue eyeshadow, and a ring in the shape of a lion's head on her index finger. I am captivated by the emerald-green and sunflower-yellow pills. Cathy weighs me, injects me with something, I don't know what, I don't ask, and counts out fourteen yellow pills for me to take home. I keep looking back at my mother, who is sitting on the brown fake leather chair in the office. She is nodding. "This is a good thing," she says. "This will help you lose the weight you gained at camp. You can't keep going like this. You are going to turn into one of those fat ladies in the circus."

I stay on the diet pills for four years, transitioning from yellow to white to my favorites: the pretty green ones. I don't lose more than the twenty pounds I lost that first month but I am afraid to go off the pills, convinced I will gain back the weight.

I am fifteen years old. My mother and I are walking to the basement. Down the carpeted steps of black-and-white circles, under the bronze angel chandelier with two dim bulbs in her hands. We turn right at the bottom and walk past my father's cubbyhole of an office. The Al Hirschfeld cartoon of Judy Garland with a single

Nina drawn into her microphone. The caricature in which my father's head is almost as huge as the wad of dollar bills he is holding.

We walk farther into the bowels of the basement—past the old black camp trunk with the brass locks, the boxes of baby books, my Garden School cheerleading coat embroidered on the right side with my name—while my mother is chattering. "I want you to see my clothes and what I've hidden."

She opens a gray metal door inside another storage room and reveals a long rack of clothes with their price tags still on them. The smell of cedar fills my nostrils, throat.

A black Chanel suit with gold buttons.

A pumpkin-orange gown with sequins.

Five silk blouses in varying colors of gray and white.

Seven dresses, all black.

Multiple pairs of pleated Mr. Dino wool pants in black, brown, white.

A dozen pairs of shoes stacked in their boxes on the floor.

The rack of clothes is so long that I can't see its end.

"Mom," I say. "My God. You have an entire store here. Look at these clothes!"

"Listen to me," she says, "because your father is not past cutting us off without a penny. It's important to get it all now. If he offers you something—anything—take it even if you don't need it or like it. The day is coming when the supply will dry up, and you don't want to be without."

I nod. Take anything, everything, whether I want it or not. Catastrophe is coming.

Later that week, I will escort my new friend Linda to the cedar closet and show her the supply. We notice a pair of white pantaloons with pink-and-black polka dots. They look like clown pants.

We decide to empty out my old clothes from the camp trunk and take them and the pantaloons to the thrift store in town.

Two days later, my mother is tearing around the house ranting about the missing bottoms to her very expensive Chester Weinberg outfit. They look like pantaloons, she says, have you seen them? I lie, say, "Of course not." I call Linda on the phone, tell her we need to get over to the thrift store immediately.

We spend hours sifting through moldy clothes: old smelly pajamas, brocade blouses, pants so big they could fit both of us. Mink stoles with heads and teeth and eyes on them. No clown pants.

"Someone," I tell Linda, "must have wanted to join the circus."

Linda tells her father, who is a famous clothes designer, about the pantaloons. He tells Chester Weinberg, who is greatly amused by our misfortune and sends a new pair of pantaloons to my mother.

I am twenty-two. "It's a group grope," I tell my mother when my boyfriend, Will, and I move to Buffalo, New York, to live with Amelia and David, the couple from Omaha, Nebraska, we met while hitchhiking. "We switch partners every Monday after dinner."

"What do you eat for dinner?" my mother asks.

"Really, Mom, that's what you want to know?"

"Well, that and what you do after you switch."

"Monday dinners are tuna fish casserole with Campbell's mushroom soup and crumbled potato chips. After dinner we have wild loud sex."

"I have two more questions," my mother says: "How good is the sex and do you have sex with the woman or is it just the men who switch?"

"The sex is great. David told me I have ice cream breasts. And I do have sex with the woman."

"Sounds exciting," she says. "I almost had sex with Margaret at the country club but I couldn't go through with it. I like penises. Anyway, I hope you are taking precautions. Why don't you come for a visit? I'd love to meet them."

The four of us drive in our red VW bus from Buffalo to my mother and my stepfather Dick's house on Long Island. Amelia and I pile out of the bus wearing tattered white lace dresses and combat boots. David and Will wear embroidered Guatemalan tunics and cowboy hats with feathers on the brim. My mother, her blond hair swept up in a French knot, her eye makeup perfectly applied, her long red fingernails like poppy petals, is waiting outside with arms outstretched to hug me.

"Come in," she says to David and Amelia, "good to meet you. I hear you are having great sex with my daughter."

A stunned silence, then laughter.

In the den, we four sit across from my mother and Dick on the taupe-and-cream-plaid couches, a fire burning in the stone hearth. Dick says, "Since this is an unusual situation, I'm thinking we should match it with what we do. Let's smoke a joint."

David and Amelia are speechless, wide-eyed. They nod. I say, "Good idea." Will has smoked grass with my mother and Dick before and says, "Go for it, Dick. Light one up."

Dick rolls a perfect joint, passes it around. We each take long tokes, coughing as we inhale. The brown-and-black-striped wallpaper gets wavy. My mother's red lipstick leaves its imprint on the white rolling paper.

"So," my mother says, "do any of you ever get jealous? Not want to make the switch?"

But before we can answer, I start to laugh and my mother, upon hearing me, laughs as well. Then we laugh harder and soon I can't remember not laughing and I am begging them, anyone, to stop laughing so I can breathe. I don't remember what happens next: if we talk or what we talk about before we wander into the kitchen and eat an entire Entenmann's coffee cake with vanilla ice cream while standing at the sink. My mother asks if anyone wants coffee.

Afterward, the grope group descends to the basement. I lead David into the cedar closet where the racks of clothes with their tags on are lined up and we writhe and moan on top of my mother's mink coat that smells of Joy perfume. My ice cream breasts feature prominently as we roll in the fur.

Later my mother says, "They seem nice, although did you notice that David's pinky toe on his left foot looked a little like a pig's toe? Also, would it be so terrible to have sex with a Jewish person?"

Four years later, I am twenty-six and living with Will in a shack on the director of Esalen Institute's property in Big Sur, California. I am reading Sylvia Plath and starving myself down to eighty-two pounds when the Esalen director catches me stealing granola from his house and tells me that if he finds me there again, he will call the police. On my way out he calls me "a leech, a sloth, a good-for-nothing, and a criminal. And," he shouts, "you might be a sociopath as well!" (I'd noticed the thick navy-blue copy of *The Diagnostic and Statistical Manual of Mental Disorders* on his kitchen table and it's possible he got carried away by seeing my hand in his granola jar, although I am certain that *sloth* and *good-for-nothing* were not clinical diagnoses.)

The day after being caught stealing, I walk down the gravel path from the shack in which Will and I live, open the door to the director's house, take a step into his kitchen, decide that stale granola is not worth being arrested for (it didn't, after all, have raisins), and turn around.

Six months later, I move to Santa Cruz and take up temporary residence in an aisle of Ray's Market in Capitola. Bulk bins had just become fashionable—it was the late seventies—and were a binger's dream. Hundreds of squares of dried fruit and nuts in one place. Vats of roasted almonds with tamari. Gallons of dark chocolate snowdrops. Whenever I grab a handful of something, there is always more of it, like loaves and fish in a bin.

I am arms-deep in carob malt balls, gobbling, chewing, swallowing, gobbling, chewing, swallowing. Suddenly, at the height of the gobble, the loudspeaker blares: "YOU! WITH THE CAROB MALT BALLS IN YOUR MOUTH! COME TO THE REGISTER IMMEDIATELY." I look up and notice the overhead mirror has caught my hands submerged in the bin and my mouth so stuffed that I cannot speak. I skulk to the register where a brawny redhead with tortoiseshell glasses is glaring at me in disgust: Pay for those now, she says, and then get out of here and don't ever come back. I want to ask how much I owe but I cannot open my mouth without spitting on the scale, so I plunk down five dollars and leave.

At Esalen or in the bulk aisle at Ray's Market, I wasn't "cruising for a bruising" as my mother used to say (well, maybe just a tinge); I was desperate to have—even if it meant stealing—what I couldn't give myself for free.

I walk home from Ray's and sit on the cold gray linoleum floor of my apartment to eat what my mother calls wetbread—a dark brown lump of uncooked nuts and grains—slathered with tahini. I take out a gallon of Breyers vanilla fudge ice cream to let it melt around the edges. After the ice cream I decide that I will eat a stack of Oreos. I scoop out the middle and put the wafers back together like my mother used to do.

I have gained eighty pounds in five weeks. (It is not difficult to gain that much weight: I eat until nauseated, wait a few minutes for the nausea to stop, then eat again. When I wake up in the middle of the night, I dreamwalk to the refrigerator and eat and cry, eat and cry.)

The phone rings. My mother says, "How are you, sweetheart?"

Since she married Dick eight years ago, my mother is no longer the mother I knew. He glows on her like a campfire and she absorbs his light, melts like marshmallows and chocolate on s'mores. From forbidding chocolate, she has become it. Now she speaks softly, murmurs that she loves me.

I am still sitting on the floor when we say goodbye. I finish eating the wetbread and begin mining the chocolate veins in the ice cream. The Oreos wait like a stack of magic coins.

Six years later, when I am thirty-three, I am sitting in Dick's dentist chair under the influence of nitrous oxide while he is drilling into my molar. I am floating in swirls of purple planets when Dick says, "So, Geneen, have you met any interesting men recently?"

Men-planets-Dick. I come back to earth, look at Dick with his magnifying glasses on, and say, "Nope, not really." He says, "Well, I am not sure who is going to be able to put up with you. You are a piece of work, Geneen."

If I weren't drunk on nitrous oxide, if his hands weren't in my mouth, if I didn't believe I was secretly damaged, I would have said: "Me? I'm a piece of work? You married *my mother*, Dick, you should know about pieces of work." Instead I believe he sees the truth; I am damaged and intense, I am sensitive and selfish and no one will want me.

Then I meet Matt. He and I are both speakers at the Association for Humanistic Psychology conference. My friend Darcy picked his photo out of the conference catalog and said, "He's the one. Meet him," and since I wasn't having any luck meeting men on my own—my last date was with a man who killed baby quail and my date before that was with a man who bit off a burglar's ear—I decide to look out for the guy in the photo. When I see him walking on a path to the conference room, I introduce myself and know within a few minutes that I am going to spend my life with him. This is unusual for me—my mother once told me that she had babies in less time than it took me to decide on anything, even which pair of shoes to buy. Matt has a gap between his front teeth, smells like fresh cinnamon rolls, and when I stand next to him, I want to say, "What took you so long?" He says he is happy to meet me, asks for my phone number, tells me he'll call in the next few days.

And so it begins.

When I introduce Matt to my mother and Dick a few months later, Matt wears an earring with a light that blinks when he moves his head. I think that my mother, with her refined aesthetic, will discount him immediately but instead she says, "I love your earring. You'll have to tell me where you got it." Fifteen minutes later, she turns to me and says, "Well, darling, it's obvious that he adores you. You found the lid to your pot."

"I did, Mom," I say. "It seems that certain people"—I look at Dick—"appreciate pieces of work."

"Touché, Geneen," Dick says.

CHAPTER TWO

The Body Project

"It's called a diet," my mother said. "Beginning tomorrow, you will cut out one piece of bread a day. And no more Good Humor Creamsicles or Chips Ahoy! cookies. You're getting fat." Age eleven.

Started sucking in my stomach and checking to see how flat it was every day when I got out of bed. Age eleven (still).

Started throwing up to get rid of unwanted food. Age twelve.

Started drinking a gallon of No-Cal diet soda a day for ten years. Age thirteen.

Took hot steamy baths and ate spinach, hard-boiled eggs, and grapefruit for three days before my next physical so that Dr. Modlin wouldn't yell at me for being fat. Age fourteen.

Limited my daily intake to three prunes, two meatballs, and a six-ounce jar of Mott's raspberry no-sugar-added applesauce for a month. Age fourteen.

Began taking amphetamines (diet pills), twice a day, for four years. Age fifteen.

Ate only hard-boiled eggs for breakfast, lunch, and dinner for two months. Age fifteen.

Took tetracycline, an antibiotic, for a year to get rid of five pimples on my face. Age fifteen.

Consulted with a plastic surgeon about straightening my already-straight nose. Age fifteen.

Ate one hot fudge sundae a day and nothing else for one month. Age sixteen.

Consumed multiple squares of chocolate-flavored Ex-Lax whenever I ate too much. Age sixteen.

Spent three weeks on a self-created all-brown diet (coffee, cigarettes, Shasta Diet Creme Soda). Age nineteen.

Followed the fried chicken diet (only fried chicken, three meals a day); my lanky boyfriend joined me. He lost twenty pounds. I gained ten. Age nineteen.

Spent a month on the all-sugar diet. Age twenty.

Went on the Atkins diet. For five months, ate a pound of turkey with ketchup for breakfast, a scoop of cold ricotta cheese with cold tomato sauce for lunch, a pound of roast beef with ketchup for dinner. Age twenty-one.

Fasted on water for ten days at every change of the season. Age twenty-two.

Fasted on lemon juice, cayenne, and maple syrup for three weeks. Age twenty-three.

Discovered health food stores: granola and yogurt clusters with pistachios. After weighing eighty-eight pounds for a year and a half, gained eighty pounds in two months eating health food. Age twenty-three.

Fasted on beet, carrot, and celery juice for a month. Schlepped it onto a plane, where I spilled it on my white pants, the seats, the trays, and my best friend's shirt. Age twenty-four.

Read *Survival into the 21st Century*. Decided to become a breatharian (someone who eats light and drinks air instead of food). Limited my daily intake to a handful of cashews and an apple. Lost fifty pounds in two months. Weighed eighty-eight pounds. Age twenty-four.

Became suicidal when I was fatter than I'd ever been and realized that I'd been on a diet or a binge every day for sixteen years. Age twenty-seven.

Read a few chapters of *Fat Is a Feminist Issue* while researching ways to kill myself in a bookstore and realized that I'd been using food for good reasons, even though I didn't yet know what they were. Age twenty-eight.

Ate raw chocolate chip cookie dough for two weeks when I stopped dieting. Switched to pumpkin ice cream after that. Age twenty-eight.

Became a vegetarian because I didn't want to eat anything that had a mother (but the real reason was that I wanted to lose weight). Age twenty-nine.

Became a vegan because I didn't want to eat anything that came from an animal with eyes (also, to lose weight). Age thirty.

Ate pounds of oat bran when those who knew said it was good. Stopped eating oat bran when those who knew said it wasn't. Ate margarine when those who knew said it was healthy. Stopped eating margarine when those who knew said it caused cancer. Age thirty to thirty-five.

Started eating meat when my doctor told me I was tired and weak from not eating enough protein. Age forty-three.

Diagnosed with osteoporosis from what the doctor said was due to a lack of childhood nutrition. Age forty-three.

Ran up and down 150 steps ten times each day for eight years until a masturbating man greeted me at the top. Age forty-five.

Broke two vertebrae from jumping on a trampoline. Age sixty.

Discovered two additional compression fractures in my spine during a DEXA scan. Age sixty-five.

Dropped sugar, alcohol, grains, and processed food. Lost twenty pounds almost immediately. Weighed 102 pounds. Age sixty-six.

Did intermittent fasting for eighteen hours a day when my doctor told me that it would prevent Alzheimer's and decrease inflammation, which contributes to osteoporosis. Age sixty-seven.

Ceased intermittent fasting after three years because the doctor said it was decreasing bone and muscle mass. She also said I would end up in a wheelchair if I didn't take immune modulator shots, which might make my teeth fall out but probably wouldn't. Age sixty-nine.

Realized I'd been sucking in my stomach for decades, which I've now learned leads to 30 percent less oxygen capacity, back and neck problems, and urine leakage while laughing, coughing, or sneezing. Age seventy.

I hear versions of the Body Project from every woman. They tell me about the cotton ball diet, the baby food diet, the all-white diet. They describe banging their hips against walls to make them narrower. Squeezing their thighs into pants that are too tight to compress the cellulite. Taking multiple hot baths a day while eating only spinach and hard-boiled eggs. Anything to be thin. Just as I have, they inflict drastic measures upon their bodies to be lovable because, like me, they believe that having a thinner body will get them closer to love and being at peace.

Pleasure with or from food is never a consideration; we do what we have to do so that one day we will be able to stop doing it. We torture ourselves with food so that one day we will (lose weight and) be able to stop torturing ourselves with food.

If the cost of being thin—which translates to being beautiful, which translates to being loved, which translates to relaxing the meanness and self-rejection with which we treat ourselves—sickens this body, we are willing to pay it.

As I wrote this list, it occurred to me that I treated my body like a wild animal that could be starved or force-fed or shamed according to my whims, which changed with every passing fad.

If I punished and shamed and yelled at my dog, Izzy, the way I punished and shamed and yelled at my body, I would get arrested for animal abuse.

If I treated my body the way I treat Izzy, I would croon at it. I would notice when it was tired and needed rest. I would speak to it kindly when it was sick or hurt. And I would stop confusing my body with all of me. There is so much more to us humans than the physical selves on which we hang our identities.

Despite the ways I've knocked my body around, my heart still beats. My lungs still breathe. My legs still walk. My body is still here, giving me chance after chance to treat it as my beloved pet.

CHAPTER THREE

The Boozy Bazaar

The neon sign of Boozy Bazaar Liquors blinked red then white as I stood shivering in the parking lot, waiting for the ten women who had signed up for my first-ever group about breaking free from compulsive eating. The liquor store was the only well-lit place in Aptos Village, a small town near Santa Cruz, and since I was living in a house on a dark country road, I'd asked the women to meet me in the parking lot. The plan was to briefly introduce myself, after which they would caravan back to the house where I was living and working as a nanny. I was twenty-eight years old.

The fly in the ointment (well, actually, it was a couple of flies, maybe a swarm) was that I did not look the way a teacher of breaking free from compulsive eating should look, even one who was charging only a dollar per session, as I was.

First: I had recently gained eighty pounds and was obviously over my natural weight. I was not chubby. I was not chunky. I was fat.

Second: It was mid-November cold in the Bay Area, and I was wearing a sleeveless summer dress because I had no other clothes, not even a coat, that fit.

Third: I had, um, curlers in my hair. A few days before the group, I'd decided that since I was fat, I'd elevate my look by putting bounce into the only thin part of me—my hair. The stylist recommended an air-dry permanent that required keeping the curlers in overnight, but when I returned to the salon the morning that the group started, a sign on the door read: "I had to go for emergency surgery. Come back tomorrow. Do not take curlers out of your hair under any circumstance otherwise it will fall out."

So, there I stood, dozens of pounds overweight in front of a liquor store with curlers in my hair wearing a flimsy summer dress on a near-winter night waving to woman after woman and saying, "Hi. I'm Geneen. I'm the leader of our Breaking Free from Compulsive Eating group . . ."

Before I could say "I will explain my appearance at the beginning of our meeting" a woman named Janet in a green polyester pantsuit looked at me and said, "You've got to be kidding," and drove away with a vroom.

Another woman with cropped black hair named Michelle looked me up then down then up then down and said, "No way I'm spending the evening with you. You have *curlers* in your hair!" I nodded. "Yes," I said, "I noticed that, too." She harrumphed, stomped back to her car, and sped into the dark night.

The remaining eight women followed me back to my living room, where we sat in a circle. After explaining the curlers and being relieved when they giggled, I told them my story of having gained and lost over a thousand pounds in seventeen years.

"I lived in diet hell," I said. "I never spent a day in which I wasn't either on a diet or a binge. I've been addicted to amphetamines, laxatives, tried every diet that came along and some I made up—my favorite being the all-brown diet on which I stayed for three weeks, consuming nothing but coffee, cigarettes, and Shasta Diet Creme Soda."

Heads nodded. Me too, me too, me too, they murmured. One woman said, "For me, it was the Sleeping Beauty diet, on which I spent most of the day in bed with the belief that sleeping burned calories. Elvis Presley liked this diet, too."

Another woman said, "And there was the Master Cleanse—lemon water, maple syrup, and cayenne . . ."

I told them I wanted to kill myself after the recent weight gain, and as I sat on the floor of the bookstore reading about guns and drugs, I saw the book *Fat Is a Feminist Issue* by Susie Orbach, read the first few chapters, and thought, Oh my God, I'm not crazy. I don't need to be locked up. I am using food for good reasons: to say what I won't say directly. I am trying to get through to myself. Oh my God, oh my God, oh my God. I am trying to get through to myself instead of trying to get rid of myself. Eating is my way to get my attention when nothing else does. My way to say "No" or "I don't like this" or "I want this but I don't want that." I stood up from the floor, bought the book, read it in one sitting at home, and the very next day stopped dieting. I was gleeful, ecstatic, confident that this was the way through the pain of what I'd been doing with food for seventeen years. Instead of believing that I was insane and out of control with food, I realized I was exquisitely sane but I was "speaking" in a language—compulsive eating—I didn't yet understand. It was as if the door to the prison had flung open and I'd stepped outside into the cool crisp air.

Two days after the bookstore revelation, a friend told me about a course called Thin Within, about natural eating and not dieting. *Perfect timing,* I thought, and signed up immediately. I drove two hours from Santa Cruz to the Holiday Inn in Berkeley. The ballroom was meat-locker cold. A tall, willowy, dyed-strawberry-blondish-haired woman wearing a red shiny wraparound dress introduced herself as Karen and announced she was our leader. I didn't like being in a room with a hundred and fifty fat people (never mind that I was one of them) and decided I was going to slink out of the room as soon as the frizzy-haired redhead took a breath. Then she said the magic words: "I eat blondies for breakfast every day."

"I am just like you," she said as she hopped around the stage like a rabbit on steroids. "I once weighed seventy more pounds and because of Thin Within," she said as she took a soulful scan around the room, "I now eat butterscotch blondies for breakfast and dinner and I still manage to stay thin."

I'm yours, Karen, I thought. *Tell me what to do and I'll do it. Jump off the Golden Gate Bridge? Fine. Walk on my knees through Haight-Ashbury? Done. Anything, as long as I, too, can eat blondies for breakfast and lose weight.*

Karen continued. "Here's how to do this: You eat whatever you want when you are hungry, and you stop when you're full. It doesn't matter whether it's brownies or broccoli, the principle is still the same. When you're hungry, you eat. When you're full, you stop. Anyone can do this. Even you," she said, locking eyes with the braided woman in front of me wearing a cobalt-blue sweater with fuzzy polka dots.

She didn't need to reel me in, as I was already waving more inner pom-poms than the Dallas Cowboys Cheerleaders after a touchdown. It was as if someone had handed me the keys to Three Bags Full, my favorite sweater store, and told me I could take anything I wanted. For free. Sugar, in its myriad forms, was all I ever wanted to eat, and the thought that I could surround myself with brownies, lemon meringue pie, ice cream, piles of cookies, and chocolate and still lose weight elated me. It reminded me of my childhood but without the guilt and shame.

My mother hated cooking, refused to do it. This, along with the fact that she and my father were never home in the afternoons or evenings, allowed my brother H. and me to fill up on frozen Milky Ways for breakfast and Swanson TV dinners for dinner. We switched between rubbery meat loaf, peas, and congealed mashed potatoes with slabs of ersatz butter, and greasy fried chicken and mixed vegetable medley dinners with pumpkin-hard carrots and green beans the color of last year's plastic Christmas trees. Our nightly ritual consisted of opening the freezer, choosing one or the other dinner. After lifting the steaming aluminum wrapping carefully and biting into the greasy leg of chicken while we watched *Leave It to Beaver* and *Bewitched*, we wore a path back to the kitchen to dive into the Yodels and Ring Dings and chocolate-covered doughnuts and coffee ice cream. Our parents were busy with dalliances at separate drinking establishments—my mother on Long Island, my father in Manhattan—which meant that our daily meal plan was based only on the whims of us children.

Karen's meal plan of blondies for breakfast fit right into my idea of what, when, and how to eat.

For six weeks, I listened to Karen's gospel about eating according to hunger and fullness cues, although when I asked about addressing the reasons why people turned to food when they weren't hungry, Karen said that wasn't part of the program. But I knew that it was. I suggested that emotions and beliefs about self-worth might be the most significant contributor to overeating, but Karen maintained that if we ate like children ate, by hunger and fullness cues, the compulsive eating would stop.

As a nanny, I was invited to sit down to dinner and eat real food every night—spaghetti and meatballs, lasagna with garlic bread and salad, chicken with zucchini and baked potatoes—with the family I worked for. I had never been part of a nuclear family in which I had a place at the table, and with my employers, I often felt as if I were acting in a sitcom about a happy family. I couldn't quite believe that people, any people, did this: that they ate real food together, talked over their days together, disagreed and laughed together. But every morning still found me eating blondies for breakfast, and, like Karen said, I was not gaining weight. When I didn't deprive myself or believe that given the chance I would chomp my way clear across the country, I no longer felt the need to binge. But I wanted to name and understand the reasons I was using food, and I believed that any woman who struggled with food and her weight would benefit from that as well. Which is half of how I found myself sitting with curlers in my hair talking to a circle of eight women.

The other half is that Ellen Bass, the teacher in the writing group I'd joined a few months before the bookstore revelation, was leading weekly writing groups for women and had edited an anthology of women's poetry. *Me too,* I thought. I can do that, too, I can lead weekly groups (for compulsive eaters) and create an anthology about breaking free from struggles with food. I'd majored in psychology, studied with Carl Rogers at the Center for Studies of the Person in La Jolla, worked at a crisis center for a few years, and figured I had a PhD in dieting and bingeing and what not to do. When, on a walk with Ellen in the hills of Aptos, I asked her what she thought about me copying her life exactly, she said, "I think it's a grand idea." And just like that, I had work and a book idea, neither of which I'd imagined six months before.

On that very first evening of the very first group, I said, "It's obvious"—I pointed to the summer dress, the curlers—"that I'm still learning. But I know that a version of this, eating according to the body's cues in combination with discovering and naming the true hunger from which we eat, is the way through the pain of this food stuff. Would you like to learn with me?"

A chorus of "Yes" and "Count me in" and "Let's go, I'm ready" followed.

We met at different venues each week. In the back of Donna's delicatessen, in Vicki's house, at Miranda's office. I kept charging a dollar a night and we kept talking about what it was like to eat when we were hungry, to stop when we'd had enough. To one another, we said aloud what we wanted to say when we were otherwise afraid to say it. "No" was a big one. "Come closer" and "I need time alone" were others.

I developed a set of eating guidelines based on listening to hunger and satiation signals. The first was one I learned in Thin Within—eat when you are hungry—and it caused a ruckus. "But that's ridiculous," a woman named Tracey with oversized horn-rimmed glasses and a short bob said. "That's just another diet some doctor made up." I laughed. "If eating when you are hungry sounds like another diet, we've strayed very far from listening to body signals. We are so glutted with one diet after another—eat fruit for breakfast, never eat fruit, only eat grapefruit, never eat grapefruit—we are awash in rules that make no sense, so much that when we finally hear something that brings us back to eating to nourish the body, we don't recognize it."

I asked the groups to bring their dinners so that we could eat together and pay attention to how the food tasted, what prompted us to eat, what prompted us to stop. And in that way, I created the next six guidelines:

- Eat sitting down in a calm environment. This does not include the car.
- Eat what your body (not your mind) wants.
- Eat without distractions.
- Stop when your body (not your mind) has had enough.
- Eat with enjoyment, gusto, and pleasure.
- Eat with the intention of being in full view of other people.

I created this last guideline as an antidote to sneaking, because I was still haunted by the memory of being with my boyfriend, Will, years before, eating a pound of cashews with my left hand, chewing on the left side of my mouth while we walked in the forest. I believed that if he really saw me, he wouldn't love me, and therefore I had to sneak. Not just cashews but my feelings, my desires, my ambitions. It was with this guideline I realized that I couldn't do anything with food that I didn't do in the rest of my life. That if I believed I had to sneak food, I also believed, without consciously knowing I believed, that I had to sneak myself to be loved and accepted.

Slowly, the women in the group started losing weight by making food free instead of paying for each bite with guilt and shame. And, for the first time, they told the truth about the machinations and the lies they'd been telling themselves and their families for years.

During the third week of the group, Michelle recounted her nightly ritual:

"I ask my husband to lock away all the binge foods: the bags of potato chips, the boxes of cookies, the bars of chocolate. He takes the key into the bedroom and hides it. After he goes to bed, I spend an hour hunting for the key. Sometimes it's inside a sock. Sometimes he hides it behind the toothpaste in the bathroom. Or in a book in the living room. I slip it ever so quietly out of its hiding place and tiptoe to the kitchen, unlock the supposedly ironclad lock, and eat and eat and eat. My husband doesn't check the quantities of food in the mornings and has no idea about my furtive nighttime prowls."

"How do you feel after you've binged?" I ask.

"Victorious. Like I really have gotten away with something big. Like I've been bad. I've been such a good girl my whole life and now, every night, I get to be bad. But I also feel sick to my stomach."

"Is there a way you could imagine being bad without making yourself sick? Is there anything you have wanted to do forever but convinced yourself you weren't allowed to do?"

She laughs. "Sing," she says. "I would like to stand in front of an audience and belt out a song."

"Is there a particular song you want to sing?" I imagine it will be a hard rock song. Imagine her wanting to wear black eyeliner and black lipstick.

She is quiet for a moment and then says, "I'd like to sing 'Puff, the Magic Dragon' by Peter, Paul, and Mary."

I ask her to sing it for us. She stands in the middle of the circle and slowly looks around, says, "Hello, you motherfuckers!" and after the laughter, she sings her song. When she is finished, the women in the group applaud. Michelle beams. "I was told I should never, ever sing. That I had a horrible voice. And I've been stuffing the desire to belt out a song for twenty years."

I know enough to refrain from commenting on what Michelle considers being bad. But at the next session, she reports that she hasn't binged again. That singing to the group was like releasing the pressure from the buildup of a lifetime of judgments about her voice.

At this same meeting, Sally mentions that during the first two weeks of the group, she had been scraping the icing off Sara Lee banana cake because her mother didn't allow her to eat either the icing or the cake ever. "So," she says, "I was eating it now because I couldn't have it then. But now that it's free, I realize that I don't even like the taste of it. It is sickeningly sweet and cloying."

When the group ended after eight weeks, seven of the eight women wanted to meet for another round of sessions. And then another. They told their friends. Their cousins. Their families. More women wanted to come. I started two more groups, charging twenty-five dollars for eight sessions, then thirty-five, then fifty. I saved enough money to move to an apartment.

. . .

In that first wave of groups, we were so ecstatic about not dieting and the sky's-the-limit eating that we were just beginning to discern the difference between what our minds wanted and what our bodies wanted. The difference between what we hadn't been allowed to eat and what would nourish our bodies. We didn't care about whether Hostess cupcakes were good for our microbiome. We didn't even know the word *microbiome*, and I suspect that if we had, we would not have cared. When you've been locked up in a dark moldy room for years and you fling the door open to the clear bright sunshine, all you want is to whoop and run and do everything you couldn't do. And this meant eating whatever we hadn't previously allowed ourselves to eat without guilt and shame.

For me, it was sugar.

During my initial forays out of deprivation prison, I ate nothing but balls of raw chocolate chip cookie dough and the aforementioned blondie brownies for weeks. I couldn't seem to get enough of eating what I'd been telling myself since age eleven that I couldn't eat. (I hadn't yet realized that I couldn't get what I believed I wasn't allowed to have—relaxation, gladness to be alive—by eating what I believed I wasn't allowed to eat; see chapter eighteen, "Eating My Words.")

I asked group members if they wanted to write essays about their experiences of compulsive eating. Many of them did. Those essays became the backbone of my first book, *Feeding the Hungry Heart*.

My first appearance on national television was a three-minute spot on *The Merv Griffin Show*, during which I was unable to get a complete sentence out of my mouth and was convinced my life was ruined. I cried for an hour in the car back to the airport in Los Angeles while the cabdriver softly murmured, "It will be okay, whatever it is, I know it will be okay." Once at home, I hacked into half a frozen cake with a hammer and ate it while standing at the sink, sobbing. The irony of catching and eating multiple flakes of cake in response to a show on which I was the expert for breaking free from compulsive eating was not lost on me, but I was desolate and couldn't think of anything to do besides eat. My second and third appearances—on *Good Morning America* and *Donahue*—did not go significantly better than the first. I stammered. I hesitated. I fumbled. Being a writer and being an author were, it seemed, two separate skills and I did not excel at the latter.

I kept writing because it brought me joy. I kept being enthralled by working with women on what, when, and how they ate. I kept refining my own relationship with food. Kept saying yes to requests to teach more and in different cities. Fairbanks, Alaska; Chicago; New York; Seattle. When the producers for *The Oprah Winfrey Show* called, nine years after my first book was published and a year after *When Food Is Love,* my fourth book, was released, I had learned to be on television and speak in whole sentences.

Suzuki Roshi, the teacher who is credited with bringing Zen to America, was once asked what enlightenment was.

"Following one thing all the way to the end," he answered.

Mother-food-love-mother-food-love. I am still following his advice.

CHAPTER FOUR

Amaryllis

It is November 2017 and I am sitting in front of the meeting room at the Mount Madonna retreat center in Watsonville, California, where I have been teaching weeklong retreats about breaking free from food-and-weight suffering twice a year since 1999. Behind me hangs a huge photograph of an Indian man with a chalk-white beard, the resident teacher here, who hasn't spoken for sixty-five years and uses a small chalkboard to communicate. During an afternoon retreat break, he wrote me a note on his chalkboard to ask what I taught there at the center. I told him my teaching was about using the relationship with food as a portal to the inner universe, and he smiled and wrote: "Tell your students not to worry. Tell them to be happy." I nodded and said, "Do you have a suggestion for how they can do that?" He smiled again. "Patience, practice, perseverance," he scribbled.

A hundred red-upholstered chairs are arranged in a chevron shape as the students file in from the breakfast buffet carrying their meals on plastic trays. They take a seat and pretend not to be impatient that we are waiting for everyone to get their food before we start eating. (I know this because a few years ago, while waiting to begin eating, a six-foot-tall, two-hundred-pound woman told me she was considering lifting me up and throwing me across the room if we didn't start eating soon, and since her threat was followed by a wave of nods and murmurs of assent, I understood she was not alone in her frustration.)

When it's time to take the first bite, a woman named Diane says, "I've eaten cantaloupe before but never like this . . . it is so good it's like a dance happening on my tongue."

I have no idea what the first person who ever saw a flower felt or said, but it couldn't have been very different from Diane's awe at tasting one bite of cantaloupe—what it was like to slow down enough to actually taste what was in her mouth—and there was ecstasy, sunsets, the sound of wind rustling poplar trees in her words. Everything, everything was in one bite.

"Sounds nice," someone else says, "but that's not what I feel at all. I'm looking down at my plate and thinking, *I took the wrong food. I should have taken the cantaloupe. Or the pancakes—not these vegetables.* I know I'm doing this to make my mother happy, but she's been dead for ten years. And the sad part is that no matter what I ate, I never did make her happy."

"My mother wouldn't let a pancake touch my lips," another woman says. "She kept telling me I would blow up like a balloon if I ate even one. So when I saw the pancakes this morning, I took eight of them. I think I'm trying to show her that she can't control me."

"And yet," I say, "it seems that you are being controlled by not wanting her to control you. Is your mother still alive?"

"Nope," the woman replies, "she has been dead for fifteen years. But I still get a feeling of satisfaction when I eat what I wasn't allowed to eat. Isn't that what you teach, Geneen? That we should eat what we want to eat? Isn't that one of your famous guidelines?"

"Not exactly," I say, laughing. "I don't think I ever said that taking revenge on your dead mother is the way to break free from emotional eating. This is a longer discussion," I offer, "but in the meantime, let me ask you a simple question: Do you like pancakes?"

"No," she says. "Not really. They're gluey and stick to the roof of my mouth. And when they aren't gluey, they are so insubstantial that when I finish eating them, I am half hungry, half flying from the quart of maple syrup I poured over the tasteless stack."

"If an adult isn't home," I continue, "when you are faced with this breakfast buffet, all you want is what you weren't allowed to have. You'll want what the kid wanted. I want cookies. I want pancakes. And saying 'Go ahead, sweetheart, eat what you want' is like telling an eleven-year-old to make herself sick."

"But what about you when you first stopped dieting?" someone shouts. "Didn't you eat what you wanted to eat?"

"I was, it's true, eating what I *thought* I wanted to eat—two weeks of raw cookie dough—when in fact I was eating what I believed I wasn't allowed to eat, but this time, without guilt."

I notice a spate of murderous glares from the women in the room and realize they are still very hungry and want to continue eating. I say, "Let's keep eating and continue this conversation another time."

An hour later, I walk back into my room, and as I slip out of my jacket, my mother calls.

"I saw the photo of you on Facebook with those Doc Martens on," my mother says. "You are fat! How did that happen?"

Without thinking, I snap back, "Actually, I'm not."

"I didn't mean you were fat. I meant that in that outfit you looked fat."

"It's still not okay to tell anyone she is fat," I say.

"I'm sorry," my mother offers. "Between the awfulness of those boots and those flowery leggings and seeing your belly, I must have temporarily lost all decorum."

I consider telling my mother how fat *she* is, how the crack of her butt hangs over her pants, how the Trader Joe's bars of chocolate she eats every night are giving birth to triple chins. Instead, and because I know I will regret being so mean, I restrain myself. "Mom," I say, "let's talk tomorrow."

As I hang up, I'm no longer an adult; I am stomping around in the bad neighborhood of my childhood, recounting the indignities of having the mother I had, reliving them over and over like a horror movie on pause-rewind-repeat: the way she lied to me about having affairs, told me I was imagining things until I distrusted what I saw, felt, knew. I pull out the old chestnut: when she dragged me across the floor by my hair, scratched my face with her nails.

Memory after memory scrawls across my mind. I am eight years old. My right ear is pressed against the chipped yellow door, listening to my mother, grandmother, and aunt talk about me: "She is mean," one of them whispers. "She is selfish. And spoiled. You have to punish her."

I lift my ear from the door. *They hate me,* I think. *I am bad, spoiled, selfish.*

I am nine years old when I hear my brother crying to my father about the Hostess Snoballs he bought with his allowance. "I bought one for me and one for Genie and you ate them both, Dad." "No, H.," I want to say, "I ate them both and I didn't think of you once." I tiptoe back to my room. I am burning with shame at being greedy, selfish, bad.

When I am eleven years old, my mother calls me into her room, tells me she is getting divorced, that she hasn't told my father yet. I start to cry. "Go to your room," she yells. "You are so selfish! All you ever think about is yourself."

Standing in the room at Mount Madonna Center, I am all the ages I ever was. Nested like the smallest Russian doll inside the big and bigger and biggest painted dolls is my certainty that I am damaged, selfish, doomed. Everything points to that. I don't like sharing my macadamia nuts with my friend Vanessa. I don't like sharing anything with anyone, so I hunch over my apple pie like Gollum over his precious ring. My precious pie. My precious chocolate.

It doesn't count that I support a friend's special-needs son, send girls in Kenya to college, and give thousands of dollars to save forests, owls, elephants, whales. I see what I believe: selfishness, damage, a bad seed.

I don't talk about these core beliefs, but they are always there, lurking, waiting for a chance to take over after a perceived rejection from a friend, a fight with Matt, an illness, or just about anything that isn't going the way I want it to go (which is, because I am replete with opinions and am fond of controlling outcomes, almost everything).

My erstwhile therapist told me that I didn't need to forgive my mother, that sometimes wounds are too deep and that my mother might die before there could be any healing or resolution between us. But I don't want that. If reincarnation exists, I don't want to come back to earth and redo the mother thing (or worse, have to go back to high school and be rejected by the popular girls, whom everyone called the Kilties after their short skirts). Kilties aside, I want to know who or what I am without my childhood conditioning. I want to know my mother's true heart and I want to resolve the conflict between us before she dies. I don't want to be eighty years old, standing at a breakfast buffet and stacking my plate with a pile of pancakes so that I can take revenge on my dead mother. As my very-much-alive mother would say, "It's not an attractive look."

When I return home after the retreat, my friend Lizzy and I meet for our Sunday morning walk on the path below her house. We are tromping through dead leaves, panting on a trail to Mount Tamalpais, when she tells me about a spiritual teacher she recently met.

"I think you'll like her," Lizzy says. "She's laid-back, very smart, and like a walking love field."

I sigh. Another teacher.

Some people go to the movies. Some people go to the theater. Some eat at fine restaurants. I sit with the spiritual teachers passing through the Bay Area (which, believe me, is enough to keep me busy every weekend of every month). I've been traveling the spiritual circuit for four decades. I have studied with Pema Chodron (loved her), Byron Katie (adored her), Eckhart Tolle (was in awe of him); I have lived in an ashram in India, gone to multiple-weeks-long Buddhist retreats where I slept in dorm rooms with ten snoring women; I attended a contemporary spiritual school integrating psychology and spirituality for fourteen years.

Each one of these teachings was helpful, some were exhilarating, but none of them dismantled the dailiness of feeling damaged. And it is here, in who I take myself to be—(i.e., sad, lonely, depressed, clear, happy) when I wake up, wash the dishes, eat breakfast, talk to Matt, talk to my mother, sit down to work—that the proverbial rubber meets the road. What I've learned in a lifetime of spiritual seeking and meditation practice has not translated into the actual experience of being alive. *So,* I think, as I walk with Lizzy, *why bother meeting yet another teacher?*

And then I remember the three amaryllis plants I bought a month ago. After I lined them up on my counter, I watched and waited for them to bloom. After a week, ten days, I was convinced I had gotten duds, decided they were the only amaryllis bulbs in all the world that were never going to bloom. *Figures,* I thought, *I got snookered again.* I was about to throw them away when I thought, *Maybe I should give them a little more time.* And then, a few days later, the buds got fatter and fatter until one morning, when I walked into the kitchen, they were open, showering their beauty on Matt, me, the kitchen sink—on anything, everything that happened to look, see, pay attention. Not duds, just dormant. Waiting for the right moment to emerge.

Lizzy and I are headed down the mountain now, passing a fairy ring of giant redwoods, a family of deer, two oak trees that have grown into each other, forming one trunk. Does it take faith, I wonder, as my feet crunch on the leaves, to keep going? It sure seems that for the longest time we are standing still, folded in on ourselves, until perhaps, suddenly, we bloom in a shower of extravagant color.

As we round the corner to Lizzy's house, I say, "Okay, then, sign me up. Who doesn't want to meet walking love?"

CHAPTER FIVE

Shopping with My Mother

My mother and I are shopping at the Healthy Food Expo in Huntington, New York, on a dolphin-blue day. I am thirty, she is fifty-two. We stop at a booth of tie-dyed turquoise-and-orange-streaked scarves made from hemp. I wrap one of them around my neck.

"Sweetheart," my mother says, "scarves should be made of silk. Always. Forget hemp. Besides, these striped tie-dyed things are beyond ugly."

I nod. She's right. Her sense of style is impeccable. We keep *shpatziring*—a Yiddish word for strolling.

Next up is the booth with a huge display of truffles. Big round chocolate globs with pink swirls on the top. The sign in front of them reads "No Sugar. Stevia Sweetened."

"Stevia?" my mother asks. "What is stevia and why haven't I ever heard of it?"

"It's a sweetener made from plants. Much better for you than either sugar or those pink packages of Sweet'n Low," says a woman with long hair under her arms and an amethyst crystal suspended around her neck.

My mother and I each take a sample. "This tastes like a rusty nail looks!" my mother exclaims. "If you are going to eat chocolate, why not eat the real thing?"

"Yeah, it doesn't taste so good," I say. "I think they might need to work on their recipe a little longer. . . ."

"You always like these cockamamie health food things. Like wet oozy fotu."

"Tofu, Mom. It's with a *T*."

"Well, it should be called fotu. Because it tastes so awful it's like it's upside down."

We laugh because although I really do like tofu, it is tasteless and her acerbic humor delights me; the way she sees things is always with an edge.

I love my mother.

I hate my mother.

I think she's gorgeous with her blond upswept hair and perfectly applied makeup and crisp clothes. Her face is a double ruffled peony in full bloom. You can't not look. You can't not be struck dumb by the wide-set eyes, the pouty mouth, the long straight nose. Men twenty years younger than she is who could be looking at me look at her. Whatever women have that command attention, that makes people go silent and gawk when they walk into a room, she has it. My friends tell me they've never met a mother like her. My boyfriends stare at her, gobsmacked, mesmerized like automatons.

In an unfortunate roll of the genetic dice, I look like my father. Round face, moon cheeks, short legs. When he and I go places together, he stops anyone—strangers on the street, salespeople—and, pointing at my face, says, "Tell me, whose face does she have? The Big B, that's who." (His name is Bernie.) My mother tells me I have my own style, that my skin is clear and my hair is shiny, but I don't care about clear skin and shiny hair. I want to look like her.

And so I love her face and I hate that it's not my face. But there's more. There's what happened between us.

We walk toward my stepfather's booth, where he is selling Xango, a juice he drinks daily that's made from the Southeast Asian mangosteen plant. He is convinced that it is the cure for everything: cancer, psoriasis, prostate disease, arthritis, but especially for their financial difficulties. Although he is a successful dentist in Manhattan like his father before him, my mother and he have blown through his retirement fund, spent their savings on trips to Anguilla, designer clothes, and diamond earrings. They have borrowed money from each of their four kids—Dick's two daughters and my brother and me—with the promise that they will pay it back with interest. They have not kept their promise to any of us. But now Dick is convinced that he got in at the top of the pyramid of this multilevel-marketing scheme and he is already counting the monthly checks he'll receive if he sells enough Xango. When I tell my mother he sounds like those old-time Fuller Brush Men who showed up at your door and tried to sell you everything you didn't realize you needed, she shrugs.

"He launches into a spiel about Xango if you even mention you have a pimple," I tell her. "When a friend called asking for me yesterday, he kept her on the phone for ten minutes, trying to sell her a case. . . ."

"He's gotten us into so much financial trouble that he might as well try to get us out of it," she says.

As we walk up to Dick's booth, he is deep in conversation with a ponytailed woman wearing jeans and a crisp white T-shirt. I hear Dick say, "Well, if you are a nutritionist, you must know about my daughter, Geneen Roth."

She gasps, backing away from Dick as if he is contagious. "I don't see how you could be so proud of yourself. I read her work and know that Geneen had a terrible childhood. A nightmare mother!"

My mother, who has heard the accusation, cups her hands around her mouth like a megaphone and, as the incensed nutritionist stalks away, shouts, "I know. I was there!"

The nutritionist keeps walking and although I laugh at my mother's brazenness, I am secretly glad that a stranger stuck up for me. It was more than I did for myself.

My mother pulls up two cobalt-blue plastic chairs behind the curtain in Dick's booth.

"Sit," she says, pointing to one of the chairs. "Let's talk."

We pour ourselves glasses of Xango, cross our legs, face each other.

"When will I have paid enough for what I did? When do you stop talking about what a lousy childhood you had and get on with the present?" she asks, her voice rising, impatient.

I feel the wall slam down in my chest. I think about saying, "When you admit that it happened," but I still don't have the courage to stand up to her.

The crack of her hand on my face when I talked back to her. Her wild eyes as she backed me into a corner. Her hands with the red-painted talons. The welts left on my arms, face, legs.

She continues, "Everyone hit their kids in those days. Bobbi and Lil and Iza and Rose. Every kid you know got hit. That doesn't amount to being beaten."

The sound of the stick on the back of my legs. The way she chased me up the stairs, one smash after another, screaming at me for being selfish. The way I didn't fight back. The way I apologized to her for being so bad that she had to hit me with a stick.

"I was so lonely as a kid," she says. "And then I met your father, who was my first boyfriend. I was fat and felt ugly and no one else had shown any interest in me. And when your father asked me to marry him, I said yes, and that I wanted two things: a television set and a baby. Nine months later you were born."

I don't want to hear what a terrible childhood she had. I want her to say, *It's true, I beat you.*

I want her to say, *I am sorry.*

I want her to say, *You're right, I was so focused on myself I couldn't focus on my children.*

It's like wanting a cat to bark, as Byron Katie says, but it will take fifteen more years before I understand that.

My mother says, "I never felt loved by my mother. She yelled at me because my fat legs rubbed together until they were raw and we had to buy expensive cream to make them better. She told me I was so fat I would never find a husband, and then when I met your father, she told me that whether I loved him or not—I didn't—I needed to get married right away because she and my father would no longer support me going to Long Island University. Then she made fun of your father. She said, 'Most people have thirty-two teeth in their mouths. Why does he look like he has sixty-four?' "

I've heard these stories before, and the same thing that happened to me when she hit me happens to me now: I become stone-faced. Steely-hearted. She keeps excusing herself for something she says she never did and it makes me feel crazy, like I made it all up. Like the time she denied having affairs after I told her I heard her talking on the phone to her lovers when I was in high school. "No," she said. "You must be hearing things."

The way she lied.

"Say something!" she says, but I am silent, withdrawn, barricaded.

"So, call me a criminal," she continues. "Call me a terrible mother when I put you on your first diet at age eleven because I wanted to spare you the pain of what I went through. I was trying to help you, for God's sake. Which is why I took you to get those diet pills when you were fifteen. How was I to know that you would get addicted to those? Or that you would spend seventeen years with an extreme eating disorder, gaining and losing a thousand pounds?"

The way she told me that my ankles were like piano stools and my thighs were like mountains and I had the body of my father's mother, whom she hated.

"God. Mothers get such a bad rap, but I have to say that in the case of my own mother, she deserved it. She was a real piece of work. She never stopped criticizing me until the day she died. Or telling me to suck up to your father because the world revolved around a stiff cock."

My nana. Her mother. Mean.

When I was twenty-seven and had just quit taking premed courses at the local junior college, I was broke and I moved in with my organic chemistry professor to work as a nanny. I was distraught, thinking of killing myself, and my nana called me a leech, a loser. Told me I was destined to fail for the rest of my life. She was no one's vision of a cheerful, supportive grandma.

I am certain that a piece of the DNA code responsible for maternal instincts was missing in our family or has wandered astray. My mother's sister June dropped her daughter, my cousin Lola, off at an orphanage when Lola was two and called my mother on her way to New Orleans to become, as June described it, "a lesbian stripper."

"You should pick up Lola within the next few days," June said. "I looked up orphanages in the phone book and left her with the first one I found. When I walked out the door, she was wailing amongst strangers."

By the time I was thirty, I'd surveyed the matriarchal lineage in our family and decided not to have children. Take a chance on becoming my mother, Aunt June, or my grandmother? No. No thank you.

I look at my mother's beautiful face and don't feel anything except that she really knows how to apply eyeliner. Which isn't to say that I don't understand her frustration. The days of hitting and screaming are over. She's been married to Dick for over a decade. She laughs at his jokes, holds his hands, speaks softly when he is around. He looks at her as if she is the sun warming the planet of him; for the first time in her life, she feels unconditionally loved.

She is not the same woman who hit me with a stick, lied, and cheated on her husband. I can no longer figure out if the years I've spent in therapy have inscribed the "I was a victim of abuse" deeper by constantly talking about it or if talking about it is releasing it. Two therapists suggested I stop talking to my mother, urged me to cut off all contact. Another therapist told me I was raised by wolves and that I was lucky that I hadn't become permanently deranged. But that might be because I tell them only half the story.

The way when I gained eighty pounds and was positive she would be disgusted at how fat I had become, she said, "You're so beautiful. You always were."

The way when I quit premed courses and despaired that I would never figure out what I wanted to do, she said, "I believe in you."

The way she loved the beauty of dinner plate dahlias and crisp white shirts.

A few months later, my mother and I are shopping again. We are at Safeway on the day before Thanksgiving after we realized we were out of cinnamon.

I threw a raincoat over my pajamas, a hat over my dirty hair, and my mother, who is always impeccably dressed—today in ironed jeans and a pale blue cotton sweater with a full face of makeup—and I walked out of the house and got into my car. Safeway is only a few blocks away, but there was no time to walk; the day before Thanksgiving is a madhouse in stores.

After driving three times around the crowded parking lot we found a space, hurried into the store, found one jar of cinnamon, threw in a pound of butter just in case we'd run out, and got in line to check out.

Twenty minutes later, I am paying for our items when the clerk looks at me and says, "Oh my goodness, I recognize you! I just saw you on television. Didn't you write that book about eating disorders and your mother's physical abuse?"

I'm stymied about how to answer her. Given how I am (not) dressed and that I am standing with my mother, I consider saying, "No, that wasn't me."

But just as I open my mouth to speak, my mother says, "Yes, that was her. She was great on that show, wasn't she?"

The clerk nods. "She really was. You really were."

I pay for my groceries, gather them in my arms, and as we are leaving, my mother turns to the cashier and says, "And by the way, I am *not* her mother."

The way she laughs at herself.

The way her relationship with Dick gave me hope that I could find a partner who looked at me the way Dick looked at her.

The way she reminded me, when I started doubting that Matt and I were right together, that every pot has a lid and she could tell by the way he looked at me that he was my lid. The way I believed her.

The way when my father was diagnosed with cancer and his wife wouldn't take him for chemotherapy, my mother showed up twice a week and carted him to his treatments.

The way she taught me to apply eyeliner.

"Darling," she says the next time she calls. "I'm sorry. I'm sorry for all the times I called you fat. And for telling you that your ankles were like piano stools.

"And there's something else I want to say before it's too late: I'm sorry for not being there for you and your brother. I was so lonely and so absorbed in my own problems that I wasn't interested in you or what you were going through. I know I was a terrible mother, just like my mother before me. Just like my sister, who dropped Linda at an orphanage when she was two and left to be a stripper in New Orleans.

"I don't want to die with you being angry with me. Can you ever forgive me?"

Forgive her.

I tell my brother that she asked for forgiveness and he says, "Yeah, right. Forget it. She's lying."

I tell my best friend from college that my mother asked for forgiveness and she says, "Don't believe her."

I tell my first therapist that my mother asked for forgiveness and she says, "She doesn't mean it. Why are you still talking to her?"

I tell my second therapist that my mother asked for forgiveness and she says, "I thought you cut off contact with her years ago."

I tell my mother I think it is brave to ask for forgiveness. I tell her that since she has always insisted that she was a good mother, I need some time—a few days, a week, a few weeks—to let her words settle.

Like everyone whose mother is still alive, I cannot remember a minute, an hour, a day without her. She is the beginning, the middle, the end of every story I've told even when I don't mention the word *mother*. She is my "root guru," the one from whom I received the direct teachings about what I needed to do, say, eat, wear, weigh, to take up space, to belong here. Even when I don't mention her, she is the unseen force behind every story I've written or told. I've grown like an antitropism away from her harsh light.

But I do not want to keep living in reaction to her.

They say that trauma is passed through five generations.

I didn't know my great-grandmother, and my mother doesn't

remember her except that she made blintzes and the members of her temple in the Bronx came out to pay their respects to her hearse on its way to the cemetery. And I know she escaped Russia during the pogroms and so she must have been traumatized by the persecution and the two years it took, over land and in freight boats, to get to Ellis Island. And I know my mother's mother was not kind, and that when my aunt June died, Lola said it was the happiest day of her life.

Forgive my mother?

What would it take? And is it even possible to drop the wall of resentment that slams down the second I hear her voice?

I think about what Lizzy told me about Coco: that she is a walking love field. I've never met a love field, am suspect that it exists, but after my mother asks me to forgive her, I decide that now might be the time.

CHAPTER SIX

The Wound Meets the Medicine

When I meet Coco, I am not impressed. It is the day after a mid-November rainstorm and the mist circling the hills of Mount Tamalpais makes me feel as if Cathy is going to be calling for Heathcliff any second. Lizzy invited her friends and arranged three rows of chairs on her deck. I take a seat in the last seat of the last row, where I always sit at events in case I feel trapped, which I often do—a leftover, I suppose, from longing to leave my chaotic childhood family.

One woman, her gold nameplate says "Melissa," arrives limping. Another woman strides onto the deck, her long blond hair waving down her back as if she were about to go surfing. Coco wobble-walks from the back door, using a cane to guide her. According to Lizzy, Coco is 90 percent blind with advanced macular degeneration—and I immediately begin to assess, judge, decide if I want to slip away. Coco's wispy hair is trying to be in a bob, pieces of it like wet feathers stuck to her face. Knobby ankles. Layers of down—vest, jacket—a teal scarf looped around her neck. *Hmph,* I think. *She doesn't look like a teacher.* I already don't like her and I begin my familiar mantra: *This isn't it. She isn't it.* I feel like the women in the workshops I lead: They sit in the back row with their arms crossed, glowering, as if to say, "Prove it to me, sister. . . ." They have tried and failed at so many food-and-weight programs, and while they have signed up to be with me, they are wary, half willing, half furious that they find themselves at yet another "food thing." They do not want to be snookered again.

Coco sits without nervousness or apology, as if she were a mountain. She doesn't need to ask for permission to exist. She begins to talk in a barely discernible Southern accent. She says, "Welcome, everyone, and thank you for coming today. I want to talk about what we all sense but don't often put into words: that we see the world through our early wounding and believe that the reality we perceive is actually the way it is."

Yeah, yeah, blah, blah, I think, crossing my legs (but careful to do it in the way my dermatologist showed me does not create varicose veins). My version of reality is crazy because I come from a crazy family. That's why I keep coming to events like this: because I still wake up in a cloud of discontent, convinced I am doing it wrong and am not the right person to be living my life.

Coco continues: "When our caretakers weren't attuned, when they were unavailable or abusive, we concluded that it was about us—I am not enough, I am damaged—and because those conclusions were unbearable, we repressed them."

Now she has my attention. I flip through some recent scenarios that at the time seemed insignificant: Matt wasn't home during a small earthquake last week. And after spending the blink of an eye being grateful nothing (e.g., my life, our house) was destroyed, I started recounting the disasters Matt had missed: two fires, the big Santa Cruz earthquake, the pipes bursting. Despite the lack of damage we experienced, I managed to decorate myself in the costume of a familiar conclusion: *I'm alone. When things fall apart, I'm always alone.*

Coco sits quietly while I flip through the Rolodex of memories of Being Done Wrong To. *Oh yeah,* I think, *the women's group I wasn't invited to last month.* When another friend told me about the group, I was standing in the kitchen. I noticed the familiar burning of being excluded. (I don't like women's groups, wouldn't have wanted to be a part of this one, but not liking something has never kept me from being hurt that I wasn't included.) *It figures,* I decided. *I am always excluded from what really matters. From where the love is.*

On Lizzy's deck, I am beginning to get uncomfortable, but I am also intrigued. I've never named the conclusions I see through. Given how much time I've spent exploring my relationship with seemingly insatiable hunger, "I am not enough" is a no-brainer. But there is also the set of long-standing beliefs that I am damaged, doomed, and irrelevant that I keep hidden. Is this what Coco means about repressing the conclusions? Almost half a century of therapy has not helped me to dismantle my "unavoidable conclusions" and I don't yet believe that Coco's teaching is the answer.

Enough of this, I think, *time to go get a chai.* I stand up, get ready to leave, convinced that I might as well accept the doomed-ness and get on with it.

"But," Coco continues, "when you push down your conclusions, they end up pushing back and getting projected out there."

Yep, I think, *and there it is, Newton's law:* For every action, there is an equal and opposite reaction. I co-opted this idea in my work as the Fourth Law of the Universe: For every diet there is an equal and opposite binge. I say it in every lecture, tell my students the story of being anorexic and starving myself on a hundred and fifty calories a day for a year and a half, after which I busted out and binged all day every day rivaling Miki Sudo, the winner of Nathan's Hot Dog Eating Contest, who ate fifty-one hot dogs in ten minutes.

Coco breaks my reverie of hot dogs and continues: "Your pushed-down and projected conclusions become the lens through which you see life—yours, others', and the culture itself—after which what you see keeps reflecting what you believe. Then we try fixing 'out there' by vowing to do better, be better, try harder, but it never works because we are not working at the level of cause."

The sun is sending shafts of light onto a pale pink two-foot cymbidium orchid near Coco. She unwinds her teal scarf, unzips her jacket, and I notice, for the first time, a stack of gold rings that look like wedding bands on the middle finger of her right hand. I don't have time to wonder about her marital status before she continues:

"What you call reality is the distorted lens of your own wounding. When you name the conclusions that drive it, you become aware that they were unavoidable but never true. With that awareness comes forgiveness for ever believing that you were unlovable or too much or damaged."

The way I tear myself apart in the middle of the night. The way I loathe myself and pretend I don't. The way I feel the self-hatred like a shadow nipping at my heels. Can Coco's process dismantle what decades of therapy and meditation have not?

Matt and I are devoted watchers of *The Vicar of Dibley*, a salty British TV series in which Jim, a church council member, responds to questions with "No. No. No. No. No." Until, inexplicably, he blurts out "yes!" *Nope*, I think now. *No, no, no, no.* And then Coco says, "All you ever experience of the world is how you are being with yourself." My head swivels and there is a clunk, a knowing she is right. A sudden hiccup of *yes!*

But then I am suspicious. I've been wrong before.

I don't want to be caught with my pants down.

I don't want to be lulled into being positive.

I don't want to believe that something bigger, happier, more expansive is possible for me.

I don't want to be entranced into believing the spiritual hoo-ha of being enlightened, of waking up, of everything is good, you are already awake.

I don't want to be snookered.

Again.

CHAPTER SEVEN

Eskimo Coat

My thrice-weekly conversations with my mother follow a similar trajectory: They start on a hopeful note, with me deciding I am going to be kind and open, and end with me wanting to strangle her. She is ninety-three; I am seventy-one.

"Hi, Mom. How are you?"

"I'm all right," she drawls.

But I hear the hook in her voice. I wait for the next sentence.

"It's boring here," she says. "My apartment is so empty since Dick died. I'm lonesome. I wish I'd had more children. The ones I never had might live closer than you do."

I feel punched in the gut and stifle the impulse to say, *Would you have been a better mother to the children you never had?*

"Sweetheart," she continues, "remember that necklace I gave

you a few years ago? I'd like it back. I miss having something to wear around my neck. Surely you have other necklaces. And if you don't want to give that back to me, what about that necklace Matt gave you for your fiftieth birthday? The one he bought at the jewelry shop on Forty-Seventh Street, with a diamond pendant . . ."

Before I can stop myself I say, "Your neck is too fat for either of those necklaces, Mom."

The better angels of my nature don't approve of my outburst but my inner five-year-old is gleeful; she's never been that blunt before. Too many memories of hitting, screaming, scratching. Of being backed into a corner and protecting her from being scratched. When my brother got his black belt in karate and caught our mother's hand on its trajectory to his face, he said, "If you ever touch me again, I will break your arm." That was when she stopped using her hands as weapons.

But today, years later, after my outburst about her fat neck, I decide to be silent for a few minutes and the conversation slides to what she is eating for dinner: scrambled eggs and a baked potato.

We say goodbye and I clomp to the kitchen shrouded in the familiar wreckage of phone calls with my mother.

I run the water, pick up the sponge, begin washing the blender. Why can't I stop lashing out? Why can't I just be kind to her? My very old mother wants a necklace. What would be so bad about sending it back to her? Why am I so resentful about being asked to send it back?

In our family, food was a weapon and things were love. When my mother gave me a sweater or a piece of her jewelry, I felt as if she was saying, "I am giving this to you because I love you," but when she asked to have it returned, I interpreted it as "I've changed my mind. You're not lovable after all. Give it back."

I am certain that a good daughter would give back the necklace, but I am, it seems, not a good daughter. Not a good person. All those years she called me selfish, all those years she said I was born damaged, she was right: I am irredeemable. A piece of shit. Stonyhearted.

Then I flip to the other side. It's her fault. What kind of mother indicts her child? Gives and then asks for things back? I still can't believe I got this waste of a human being for a mother, the one who, by her own admission, said she was never interested in anyone but herself.

I start making a mental list of the things she's given and wanted back over the past twenty years: The picture frames, the sweaters, the purses, the boots. The necklace with the charm in the shape of a heart that I wore every day. The brass wall sconce my father left me that she said she would send to me. I picked out a place for it in our house but when I asked her for it, she said she'd changed her mind. "I want it," she said, "you don't need it."

What remains forever branded in my memory is the emerald-green quilted jacket with fake-fur trim that my mother bought for herself during a family outing to the Ella Lou Ski Shop on Ditmars Boulevard in Queens. We didn't usually have family outings and we didn't ski, but my parents were expert shoppers, and walking down aisles and buying things was a way to spend Sunday afternoons. Better than going to a museum, because you can't buy paintings from MoMA but you can buy jackets from a ski shop.

My mother pranced around the store with her blond hair wisping from the hood, her bright pink lipstick defining her face. I was in fifth grade, and we'd just learned about Eskimos—how they live in igloos and kiss with their noses and hunt seal and whales for food. I told my mother she looked like an Eskimo. (Later, much later, we learned that the term *Eskimo* is offensive; now they are called the Inuit.) But what I really thought was that I wanted to look like an Eskimo, too. I wanted to look exactly like my mother. "I would like to look like an Eskimo, too," I said to her and she nodded. "I will give this to you for your next birthday," she said—and I started counting the days until August 30.

In mid-August, the dreaded Lola, my first cousin on my mother's side, arrived to spend two weeks with us and I watched as my mother became Angel Mother to her. Nicer than June Cleaver on *Leave It to Beaver*. She called Lola *darling*, giggled with her, and never once yelled at or hit her.

I hated Lola. Her dark brown eyes, her thick curly hair. I hated that she got the mother I wanted. I wanted her to leave, to never come back, to die.

With only fourteen days left until my birthday, Lola saw the Eskimo jacket and told my mother she liked it.

"Here," my mother said. "Take it."

I was standing in the kitchen, near the pink linoleum table with gray flecks. My mother and Lola were in the adjoining dining room, heads close together, unaware of my presence. At first, I was convinced I didn't hear correctly. She couldn't, *she just couldn't,* have told Lola she could have my birthday present. My stomach churned, my heart thumped. It was never a good idea to argue with my mother. Bad things happened. But I lost my usual restraint. I couldn't hold it all in and arrange my face into a wall the way I usually did.

"But you said I could have it!" I blurted. "You promised to give it to me for my birthday!"

They both turned to look at me.

"Do you only ever think of yourself?" my mother asked, voice rising. "For once, think about someone else. Think about Lola. There are no words to describe you except *selfish, selfish, selfish.* Now go to your room."

And then there were my three favorite rings, which together formed a flower, suddenly gone from my jewelry box. I was a chunky new girl in school that year—ninth grade, fourteen years old—and Robert Horowitz puffed up his cheeks every time he saw me. Fred Lasky showed up outside my bedroom window at ten p.m. and called me fat, ugly, balloon-face. Another girl, Betty, pulled my skirts, made scary faces at me when she saw me, followed me home, telling me I was a loser. But the rings. I invested magic in those rings and told myself they would bring me good luck because anyone who saw them would think that the girl who wore them was as pretty and cool as those rings were. I searched for them under the box, the bed, on the floor. No rings. I asked my mother if she'd seen them. No, she hadn't.

Six weeks later, the rings reappeared in my jewelry box with holes where the petals and pearls once were.

"Mom," I said, "my rings appeared again. Do you know what happened to them?"

"Oh, those," she said, "my friend Lil decided she liked them and wanted to wear them for the past few weeks."

"You told me you didn't know what happened to them," I said.

"I forgot," she said.

"That isn't fair," I said.

"Life isn't fair," she said. "Go bang your head against the wall and when you stop, you'll feel better."

Each time, with each item of mine that she claimed for herself, she'd say, "I need it more than you." If I'd balk—"Mom," I'd say, "it feels terrible to be given something and then asked for it back"—she'd say, "It's just like you, isn't it, to only think of yourself. Send it back. It's mine." And like a girl who wanted to prove she was good while believing she was bad, I returned everything.

I stand at the sink, marinating in the feelings, the hurt, the outrage. *I'm lucky I am not a serial killer,* I think, *although I bet some of them had better mothers.* Then I remember that Charles Manson's mother traded him for a can of beer. Even in my frothed-up state, I recognize that's worse than asking for a necklace back. I drop the serial killer narrative.

The dishes are done. An owl hoots, my dog barks, the ruby-red amaryllis shouts, *Look at me. Look, look, look at beauty.* I remember lines from a David Whyte poem, "Everything Is Waiting for You":

> *Put down the weight of your aloneness and ease into*
> *the conversation. The kettle is singing*
> *even as it pours you a drink . . .*

But I don't want to move from my position. I love hating my mother. And I hate hating my mother.

PART TWO

Sugar on Shit

CHAPTER EIGHT

Sugar on Shit

The mist has given way to splashes of sun on Lizzy's deck. Coco asks if there are any questions. Before I realize what I am doing, I raise my hand. She nods, acknowledging me, and I think, *Uh-oh. This was a mistake.* But I plunge ahead, making a running jump off the diving board before I know how to swim.

"I am having trouble believing that it's possible to stop identifying ourselves with our wounds and to know ourselves as awareness that sees them. I'm through hoping for change, which I have done for decades without much to show for it, and I don't want to want what is impossible to have. I don't want to be snookered again."

She throws her head back and hoots with laughter, leans forward in her chair, looks straight at me (or, since she is near blind, looks as if she was looking straight at me), and says, "*Snookered* is such a great word. And I understand not wanting to believe that it's possible to dismantle the wounds and feel the freedom when you do. But how about you tell me what you mean by being snookered."

"I mean believing that it's possible to love without getting slammed."

Coco nods, says, "I use a process called the Six Steps, in which you start with a trigger from the current situation and follow it to a feeling, an earlier similar situation, and a conclusion you made about yourself. Are you willing to do that with me, now?"

I say a reluctant yes because I figure that the only thing I have to lose by doing this work in front of thirty people is the pretense that I am sane and enlightened.

"Thank you for your courage," she says. "Now, what is your current trigger?"

I tell her that I can't get beyond blaming my mother for pretty much everything, but particularly for the years I spent believing I was too fat, losing and gaining enormous amounts of weight, and always hoping that if I were thin enough, I'd be good enough for her to love me. "I know I'm not alone," I say. "I am not sure I know a woman for whom the connection between body size, self-worth, and mothering isn't emblazoned in their brains, but that doesn't make it easier to dissolve."

Coco nods and says, "Although that might be true, what you are feeling now is about you, only you. It is not about your mother."

"I don't like that," I tell her. "And I don't even see how you can say that. My mother beat the shit out of me."

"And that might be true," she responds, "but it is what you

concluded about yourself from the situation with your mother that is causing so much suffering now."

Fuck, I think. *How did I get myself into this? And can I leave now?*

"This," she repeats, "is about you. Are you willing to at least try this? If it doesn't work, if you don't like it, if it's too painful, you can always pick up blaming your mother again."

I nod and steel myself. I do and I don't want to let go of blaming my mother.

"Tell me your earliest memory of feeling snookered," she says.

"Really?" I say. "You really want to go there? I thought this was about me, not about her, and if I go back to an early memory, it will be about her."

"You can't heal this unless you feel this. And you are not going to feel it by transcending it. Also," she adds, "it might seem like it's about her, but it's not. It's about what you concluded from the situation."

I go back to an early memory. Going back is like scratching an itch too hard. I get to have some perverse satisfaction from how awful it was. I might even show Coco that she is wrong, that my mother was a monster. But it's painful to relive, in part because I am still convinced that I was a victim.

"So," Coco says, "tell me about being snookered."

I close my eyes and flip back as if I were watching a movie of the years on Eightieth Street in Jackson Heights—and my dread of night.

I was eight, nine, ten years old and sitting on the edge of my mother's bed watching her get dressed, which was an hour-long process. A tight red suede skirt and jacket one day. A black sequined dress the next day. From my perch on her brown quilted bedspread, I watched her put on "her face": the careful application of eyeliner on the upper and lower eyelids. A layer of foundation, then powder, then a circle of blush powder on the apples of her cheeks.

"Where are you going, Mom?"

"None of your business."

"When will you be back?"

"None of your business." Her voice is rising, getting tighter, angry.

"But, Mom, I can't sleep when you aren't home."

"That's too bad for you."

"But, Mom," I'd say, and she'd turn from the makeup mirror and bark, "Go do your homework. Go watch TV. Go do something, anything. But don't eat. And for God's sake, stop asking me questions."

After reviewing herself in the mirror one more time, she'd slip on a pair of five-inch heels and *click click click* out the front door.

"Over and over, every night, I'd watch, I'd ask, and every night, I would feel snookered by love. Caught in the act of wanting what I couldn't have. Ashamed to want a mother who didn't want me. And when I'd lie awake at two, three, four a.m. with neither parent home, I'd promise myself that I would stop wanting, hoping, asking, I'd give up believing that something bigger and happier was possible for me."

A pot of spiral succulents with small gold eyes is gleaming in the bright light, and for a second I imagine they are staring at me. (*Again?* they sigh. *You're telling the story of those miserable afternoons on your mother's bed again?*)

"What did you feel?" Coco asks. She pulls her arms out of her down jacket, crosses and recrosses her legs.

"Shame that I wanted a mother who didn't want me," I answer. "Snookered by opening my heart and then getting slammed."

"What kind of child," she asks, "would be left by her mother every night?"

"A child that is irrelevant. A child that is unlovable. A child that doesn't matter."

"So, your conclusion is that you don't matter—is that correct?"

"Uh-huh."

"There wasn't any way to avoid that conclusion," she says. "The person you depended on for love neglected you. But from this perspective, as if you were simply watching what happened, you can look at the child and see there was no way she didn't matter, that it couldn't have been true."

I sort of get it: My conviction that I don't matter is the lens through which I see almost everything—it's there when I wake up in the morning, it's there like a song throughout the days, it's there when a friend rejects me.

But.

My mother-stories are my calling card, and letting go of blaming her feels like letting go of what makes me me. It is so familiar, so comfortably uncomfortable.

Coco says, "It sounds as if this conclusion is a basket of 'I don't matter' conclusions and that it is well ensconced, backed up by multiple incidents."

Recounting these memories is like watching a sad movie for the ten thousandth time and I feel exhausted. But then it occurs to me that all the ways I define myself, that my students define themselves, that anyone, anywhere defines or identifies themselves, are conclusions that we made up from what happened in childhood.

That the conclusion is my creation, my interpretation, and not "objective reality." This idea is so radical that I can't consider it for long; I am still, it seems, quite fond of blaming.

"I'm not saying that your mother was not self-absorbed and abusive," Coco says. "I'm saying you interpreted her behavior to mean something about you that was not true and you are still seeing through that conclusion. Telling yourself you're not affected by what deeply affects you or pretending that it's over, fine, in the past is like putting sugar on shit."

I shift in my seat and begin bunching the fabric of my pants through my fingers. My last therapist told me there was nothing wrong with not forgiving my mother. "It is a wonder you still talk to her," she said, reinscribing the belief that I was a victim of mother-neglect. But aside from the awful thought that I will have to come back to Earth again in the next life as her child if I don't forgive her, I notice that as I listen to Coco I feel as if a caboose has unhitched from the long line of railway cars and is gliding, wild and free, down the tracks.

"When you see that you made up your conclusion, that it is your interpretation of what happened and not what actually happened," Coco interjects, "you can forgive yourself for believing that you didn't matter, that you don't matter. Because when you are aware that these beliefs couldn't have been true—no child is inherently unlovable—you can turn to yourself with the love you were waiting for. The love you've been waiting a lifetime to receive."

"That's so schmaltzy, Coco," I say. "And the gimmick of turning to myself with the love I didn't get is well-worn, well-used, and clichéd. I did this forty years ago with my first therapist."

"Sometimes," she answers, "clichés are cliches because they

are still rooted in truth. And despite what you call schmaltz, the ability to be on your own side—something I am guessing that you have rarely or never done—changes everything. It's not that the adult-you meets the child-you; it's that you as awareness, as presence, become the one you were waiting for."

I think about what it means to be on my own side, to stop rejecting myself by comparing myself to other people and believing I am living the wrong life. In Coco's words, the true snookering is that I keep leaving myself—and breaking my own heart. "Seems as if you are describing love without snookering?" I ask. She nods. My mind quiets. The trance of how terrible, how awful, how hopeless this is (and I am) breaks. A tiny whoop of laughter escapes from my mouth—enough mirth for me to approach Coco and ask if I can set up a phone session with her the following week. "I'd love that," she says, and I believe her.

CHAPTER NINE

The Body Project II

During my first phone session with Coco, and as a way of introducing myself and letting her know I'm not a run-of-the-mill dieting wimp, I recount my Body Project. I tell her that every woman I've worked with has a similar list.

Coco says, "Oh, sweetheart. The lack of kindness you've shown your body is stunning. You've never been on its side."

I roll my eyes, which she doesn't see because we are on the phone, and say, "You sound like a New Age aphorism: Be kind to your body and your body will be kind to you. Besides," I continue, "I thought I *was* being kind to my body. Everything I did to my body I did for me. It was all about being wantable, lovable, as beautiful as possible given the limitations of having thin wispy hair, eyes that are too close together, and ankles like piano stools. Striving and pushing, taking drugs and reciting mantras, were about one thing only: surviving the self-hatred that was hovering, waiting for a chance to take over the controls. Everything I did, I did to keep myself from drowning, which seems like kindness to me," I retort.

"You keep treating your body as if it were you. As if fixing it will fix how you feel about yourself."

But. But. But.

"An eating disorder," I spurt, "is an expression of the conviction that I am my body. I am the size of my thighs. The less I weigh, the more I am."

"True," Coco says, "but that is a lie. And just because you believed it and just because the culture supports it and just because it gets blasted at you from every magazine, movie, TV show, and social media site doesn't mean it's true. What they don't tell you, and what is true, is that you are the awareness that sees this body. You can't be your body and also be the awareness that describes this litany of what you did to it. You are only and forever the awareness itself."

"That is radical," I say. "So radical that some therapists might call it dissociation."

I've heard other teachers say this same thing: You can't describe what you are feeling if you are the feeling itself. Something has to be outside the feeling to even describe it. The painter is not the painting. Thoughts and feelings come and go, but what sees them—awareness itself—remains unchanged. You are the noticer, not what is noticed. Which means that I notice this body and what I did to it, while knowing myself as the awareness that notices it.

"If I knew that I was the awareness, I'd be enlightened," I tell Coco.

"Exactly," she says.

For so long, my work has centered on the body as if it and I were the same. The push for thinness, the judgments about thighs, when, how, and how much to eat. How to stop punishing and depriving this body.

"That's the therapists' mistake," Coco says.

She continues: "Until now, your body has taken the hit of your woundedness, which means you've spent a lifetime rejecting and abandoning it—and yourself."

Ouch. I watch the silent replay of the fasts, the drugs, the broken vertebrae, the incessant push to look a certain way so that I could one day relax into being who I thought I needed to be. All of it based on shame.

"The body-mind identification is at the heart of all suffering," Coco says. "When you know that you are what is seeing the body, that you are what is aware of your thoughts, the suffering unravels because you realize that you are not at risk of disintegrating if you gain five pounds."

But believing I am my body is the foundation on which I've built a sense of self, who I take myself to be. Letting go of that belief feels like cutting the strings that tie me to almost everything: friends, work, family. If I'm not my body, then I'm not the perceptions of my body. I'm not the sensations of my body. I'm not the size of my body. And if I am not any of those, what's left? Coco would say, "What's left is what has always been there. It's the answer to the age-old question *Who am I?*"

It doesn't matter that I mentally know that I am the awareness in which all feelings, sensations, and thoughts arise; until it's my tangible experience, until I feel and believe it, telling myself I am not this body means nothing to me.

Before now, the list of what I did to my body didn't register as being unkind to myself. I thought I needed to be unkind to be kind. To turn against myself to turn toward myself.

I was wrong.

CHAPTER TEN

Cancer Ruined My Thighs

When I was sixty-four, five years before I met Coco, my doctor suggested that for one month, I stop eating anything that didn't look like itself as it grew, which included everything I usually ate or drank. Chocolate, crackers, tortillas, coffee, milk, cookies, ice cream. He also said to stop eating mangoes, papayas, and pineapples. Anything starchy. Anything that could spike insulin. Anything delicious.

It was, he said, a way to decrease inflammation—the catchword that is allegedly responsible for almost every disease—and to see if we could understand what was stealing minerals from the density of my bones, a process that, according to my endocrinologist, was "catastrophic." It never occurred to me that following this diet would result in weight loss; I'd been at the same weight for twenty years and was fine being not-thin-not-fat.

I lost fifteen pounds in three seconds.

I finally weighed what the cool girls in high school weighed and looked like the Kilties looked. I weighed so little that there was no way I could have been called fat or round or chubby. My thighs were like bamboo sticks. My moon face looked like the air had been sucked out of it. My friend Joanie started crying when she saw me because she thought I was dying.

Me? I thought I looked stellar.

I stayed on the program longer than recommended because, I told myself, I wanted to prevent degeneration of my spine: I had fractured four of my vertebrae, and I didn't want a fifth to break when I bent down to make the bed. But the real reason I stayed on this eat-only-what-looks-like-itself-as-it-grows plan was that I was not about to give up this long-coveted body size that I hadn't realized I'd coveted. For the first time in my remembered life—except when I was anorexic and still thought I was too fat—no one, not one person, not even me, not even my mother, could call me fat.

Then, when I was sixty-eight, my left breast was diagnosed with cancer, which underscored the determination to stay on the diet because, as most doctors will tell you, "cancer likes sugar, so stay away from it." But after the surgery, the radiation, and the ongoing medicine to prevent recurrence, my body was fatter, thicker, droopier. My jeans no longer fit me. My arms bobbled. I had muffin top where once there was tautness, a belly so round that a teacup could have balanced on its top. And although I was grateful that I was not dying of breast cancer, I was disappointed that I no longer looked like an aging Kiltie. The fifteen-year-old in me finally got what she believed was going to make her lovable, hip, gorgeous—being skinny—and cancer ruined it.

In *The Bright Hour,* a memoir of living with metastatic breast cancer (that she eventually died from), Nina Riggs wrote that the last words her dying-of-cancer mother uttered were "I'm so fucking fat." And my friend Sophie tells me that in the last few months of her mother's life, her mother refused to eat mint chocolate chip ice cream, her favorite food, because she didn't want to "die with fat thighs."

A woman recently wrote to me that "at age seventy-eight, I am wondering if I will *ever* lose this obsession with weight loss. I continue to be twenty-five or thirty pounds overweight and wake up every day determined to take control some way or another, but by the end of the day, I haven't followed through. Time seems to be running out for me to love myself. . . ."

Not cancer, not aging, not even dying pierces the trance of the cultural imperative to be thin and the self-hatred that accompanies it.

During the precancer years when I was on my eat-only-what-doesn't-taste-good diet, I looked like I was dying of a wasting illness—the medical term is *cachexia.* I knew that my thinking was distorted; I kept telling myself that I was no longer fifteen and that having twigs for legs was not attractive—and that my fondness for twig thighs contradicted everything I'd taught and written about—but the conditioning was so entrenched that I was exultant. I felt a curious mixture of revenge against those long-ago people who told me I was fat—most of whom (I looked it up) are now dead—and elation because I had what I never thought I could have: spaces between my upper thighs and my calves, size two jeans.

The night my left breast was diagnosed with cancer, I heard a voice that said, "This cancer is about love," and since I'd never heard voices (or seen angels), and since I roll my eyes at big sweeping statements about love, I was startled enough to pay attention. In the pitch-black dark, I said, "What does that mean?" The voice didn't answer, but I already knew it meant that being diagnosed with cancer offered a chance to stop pushing myself. To be easy, tender, kind to myself. I was sixty-eight years old and still driven to achieve, acquire, become, still in thrall to a harsh voice from forty years back that surfaced when I used to binge: *Again. Harder. More.*

For a while after the diagnosis, a year perhaps, I didn't want to move with the speed I'd once moved; I lived and walked and talked at half my previous pace, at what the Jungian psychologist Marion Woodman called "soul speed."

Cancer was my get-out-of-jail-free card. Elizabeth Wurtzel, author of *Prozac Nation,* said, "I have been the most impossible person my whole life, and now I no longer have to make excuses. Now I'm just like, 'I have cancer.' And people are like, 'By all means, ruin our lives. Wreck the house.' " So, in an odd way, cancer relieved me of the need to be better than I thought I was.

But then my body started to change. The flap, the bobble, the belly. And the lack of kindness that accompanied it. Cancer, I decided, ruined my thighs.

And since it is I whom people call or write for help with minds that are possessed by the culturally induced thin hypnosis, I began to wonder whether the years of writing and teaching about sane relationships with food were a lie.

Having a life-threatening illness and surviving it only to say that it ruined the size of my thighs because I no longer looked like I was dying was appalling. But I was so used to talking to myself that way, I thought it was normal. I also thought it was true.

Before cancer, I had my dream thighs.

After cancer, my thighs were mushy and waggly.

Before cancer, I had shapely, muscled thighs.

After cancer, my thighs hung loose and flabby.

So, cancer did ruin my thighs.

To which any sane person would say, "So what? Who cares about your thighs? You had cancer, for God's sake."

Cancer. Thin thighs. Cancer. Thin thighs.

The real question, of course, and maybe you are a lot smarter than I am and already know this, should have been: Why did I want thin thighs?

I didn't want thin thighs because they were attractive.

I didn't want thin thighs so I could fit into size two jeans or triumph over the now-dead people who once taunted me. (Well, except for the bully in high school who called me Pregnant-Faced Cow. Him, I wanted to step on.)

I wanted thin thighs because I thought having them would fix what was broken. The self-loathing that was so deep I was ashamed to talk about it even to my husband. The certainty that when it came down to it, when you scratched away the glitter and the top five layers of sheen and brightness and trying to be a good person, you'd find a damaged, selfish waste of a human being.

I wanted thin thighs because I was still transfixed by the belief that something out there could fix what was in here.

I wanted thin thighs for the same reason that I ever wanted anything—a partner, a new car, or a trip to Hawaii—I thought they would dissolve the discontent, the vitriol, with which I talked to myself, and only happiness would remain.

I see this pattern continually with students: They believe that the cause of their pain is their weight and that when they lose weight, they will remove the pain. But then they lose weight and are happy for ten minutes, after which they feel let down, lost, uncertain about what to do and where to put their attention now that their goal has been reached. One woman once told me, "My Weight Watchers badge read: 'I lost ten pounds.' And underneath it, I wrote, 'And I still feel like crap.' I wanted it to make the pain go away. It didn't. And I don't know what to do now."

Often, my students gain the weight back so they can look forward to losing it again. They wrap themselves in the illusion (again and again) that something tangible—a number on a scale, the size of their thighs—can fix what is broken.

But, as I am finding out, the pain is caused by the wounds we are looking through and not what we are looking at.

I met Coco a year after I finished breast cancer treatment, five years after I'd begun the anti-inflammatory diet—which I was still following because I didn't want to eat or do anything that cancer liked. My breast felt like it was turned inside out and was in continual dull, aching pain. The surgeon had sewed up the lumpectomy area like I sewed the pockets on my apron when I was in fifth grade home economics, which is to say, bunched, crunched, and folded in on itself. My thighs were no longer thin and I didn't like it or them. After that first meeting with Coco, I realized that trying to replace the meanness of "cancer ruined my thighs" with its opposite of "I love my thighs, I love my body, it survived cancer, isn't that fabulous" would be like picking up the other end of the same stick and tugging. It would be like trying to solve the problem from the same level of thinking that created it, to paraphrase Einstein. Change doesn't happen by affirming what you wish to change and refuting what doesn't serve you. As Coco said, it's like putting sugar on shit.

I know, without a doubt, that happiness is all we ever want. It is why astronauts soar into space. Why rock climbers risk their lives. Why we travel to far-flung lands. Why we starve ourselves. Why we get drunk. Why we eat chocolate truffles. Why we go to therapy. Why we meditate. Why we watch cute animal videos. Why we buy new sweaters or gadgets. Why painters paint. Why writers write.

We know, somewhere we know, that happiness is possible, that it is waiting to be discovered if only we can find it, if only we can get out of our own way. And we remember a time, either when we fell in love or watched a sunset or met our newborn child or were six years old and full of beans, that we were perfectly, unutterably happy. Nothing was wrong. Nothing was missing.

We sense. We glimmer. We ache for the possibility. But we don't know how or where to find it. And so, we settle.

For a job that bores us.

For a friendship we know is unrequited.

For a partner we don't love.

For the latest shiny object.

Each time we get the promised thing/person, there is a quiver of hope that maybe this time it will work, followed by the letdown that it didn't, followed by a stab of despair, followed by a wham, a get-me-outta-here, this hurts, followed by a piece of pie or a drink or an attempt at inner peace through impulse buying followed by a tirade of shame and meanness followed by a quiver of hope in the next promising thing or person or situation.

. . .

It seems that breaking the cycle means a slow dissolve of the conclusions that fuel it.

The Indian sage Nisargadatta told his students to "get back. Go back. And further still."

To where? To what?

Not to the situations that we eat to avoid.

Not to the loneliness we feel when we walk into a dark empty house at the end of the day and ice cream beckons.

Not to the first time our mothers told us we were chunky and needed to lose weight.

Not to being rejected by the Kilties. Or to being left by our first boyfriend.

Not to being a victim. Not to blaming. Not to the trauma, the abuse, the abandonment, but to what we concluded about ourselves when those things happened.

I know (or I think I know) that I am seeing the world through my conclusions, but I am still doubtful that freedom from the wounds and falling into the clarity of living without my conditioning is possible for me. My resentment toward my mother, my self-loathing, my relationship with food and the size of my thighs feel tangled together, wrapped inside one another. I'm willing to untangle them, to keep untangling them, because it seems that the alternative is living on a low simmer of blame and self-hatred. Not exactly a recipe for joy.

CHAPTER ELEVEN

The Bad Neighborhood of My Mind

I continue working with Coco, having an hour-long call with her every other week. These conversations feel like a meandering path through dappled woods with stops to look at ducks and eat peanut butter sandwiches. She is laid-back, unassuming, and I am attached to the drama of being the victim of a mother who didn't want to be a mother. I can hear it in my voice, how, when I tell Coco about my past, there's a rise, an indignation, a *Can you believe this happened? Isn't it outrageous that she did that?* in my voice.

It vexes me that Coco has not uttered a word of judgment. I want her to hate my mother. Instead, she talks to me about conclusions. About the necessity of uncovering them before putting them down.

"Sweetheart," she says for the hundredth time, "this is about you, not your mother," to which I say, "And then my mother walked out the door . . ."

She says, "This isn't about what happened then. It's about what you are telling yourself now," and I say, "And then she threw a pumpkin pie at my father and he walked out the door . . ."

I pour over Coco's attempts to defuse my indignation like a chocolate shell topping over vanilla ice cream. I am hardened in my conclusions. Victimhood is my middle name. If I knew another way to disappear the discontent, to wake up happy and alive, I'd do it.

After six months of phone sessions, a friend offers Matt and me two weeks at a condo on Kauai, where Coco lives. It is March 2021, and Matt and I have not traveled since the beginning of the pandemic. We are reluctant to get on planes, to be in crowds, but the allure of Kauai, where we've spent sun-drenched, utterly happy vacations, and the chance to sit with Coco in person outweigh the fear of travel.

A day after our arrival, I drive to Coco's cottage and walk up a steep driveway lined with bushes of showy pink bougainvillea so profuse that it feels like they should have to ask for permission to be this gushingly alive.

I remember now that I feel this way whenever I visit Kauai: that if heaven were a place, it would be here—where the sky is hard blue, the sunrises can't decide whether to leave you breathless with rainbows or plumes of marmalade and crimson or both—and I can't believe anyone actually gets to live on this island. (Who gave them permission to live in heaven? I wonder. To spend their days in such lushness?) It reminds me of the first time my father visited me in Santa Cruz. "No one should live here," he said. "This is a bungalow town; it's not real life."

I stare at the draping bougainvillea, want to imprint its color behind my eyes, keep it ready for when I feel drab, gray, discontent. I knock on Coco's etched glass front doors.

"Come in, sweetheart," I hear her call, and there she is, sitting on a beige plaid couch, her hair like feathers. A face as open as a summer day. She says, "I'm so happy you are here. Come sit on the couch with me." She pats the cushion next to her and I take my shoes off, settle myself among her pillows.

Coco has a white flimsy scarf wrapped around her neck, a flouncy navy blue-and-white Hawaiian-motif shirt with a coffee stain visible near her right breast.

"Tell me," she says. "How are you?" It takes exactly three seconds before I launch into the story of what happened with my mother before I left.

"She asked me to send back a pair of boots and a sweater she'd given me a few months ago."

"And why does that bother you?" Coco asks.

"Because it brings back the other times she's asked for things back—and what she told me."

"I know we've talked about this, but let's keep going with the giving-and-taking pattern. Go back to another one of those memories," she says. "Tell me what you believed about yourself then."

And so I go back.

Fifteen years ago, my mother gave me a jacket lined with her mother's old mink coat. It was black poplin on the outside, a huge zipper, a balloon shape. I wore it every day in the winter. It smelled like her, like Joy perfume. When I wore it, I felt as if I were wearing a good mother, as if I were the kind of girl a mother could love. A girl as sweet as tuberose and gardenia.

"I'm cold," my mother said one day on the telephone, "please send me the jacket back."

"I like that jacket, Mom, I wear it every day."

"That's too bad about you," she said, her voice brittle as ice chips. "I'm cold. I want it back. And isn't it just like you to only think of yourself. To want to be warm when I am cold. You were always like this, only thinking of yourself."

I tell this to Coco and she asks, "What did you conclude about yourself then?"

"Something is irreparably wrong with me. I'm damaged. A bitch to my bones." I feel as if I were letting her see the black stain at the back of my heart.

"Can you forgive yourself for believing that you were ever worthless, a bitch to your bones?"

"Forget it," I say. "I don't want to go back into the Buddhist version of forgiveness. I've tried that dozens of times: imagining the person who hurt me and saying, 'I forgive you for anything you did knowingly or unknowingly that caused me pain.' Whenever I've done it, I end up feeling like a forgiveness failure, which makes me feel even meaner."

"This isn't about the people you tried to forgive," Coco says. "Nor is it about condoning anyone's behavior. This is about forgiving yourself for trashing yourself by believing the lies based on your conclusions. When you see, really see, that what you think happened didn't happen the way you thought it did, there is nothing to forgive."

Blah blah blah forgiveness. I've never met a forgiveness process that melted my steely heart.

"Think about it for a minute," Coco says, "a child is standing at the end of her mother's bed and is told that her parents are getting divorced. She cries like any child would. She is frightened about what will happen to her. Does that make her irredeemable? Selfish?"

"So we're back to the inner child thing again? If I had the money I paid a posse of therapists to do ineffective inner child work, I could buy a small island. Is it ever time to stop going back to the inner children?"

Coco says, "It is, when they stop hijacking your present-day life. When you stop behaving as if you were one of them."

CHAPTER TWELVE

Wet

I want to change the subject of rooting around in conclusions for a moment and tell you how I know that inconceivable change is possible. Let's take a break from the bad neighborhoods of our minds, prepare to be happy, and live as if we were Matt, my husband, who, with each day, answers my question of "How are you?" with "Never better."

A broken-down 1960 California ranch house near San Rafael was on the market for five years without an offer until Matt saw it and decided we could live there. The house didn't have heat. It rained more inside than out, and the leaky swimming pool in the backyard was thick with algae. Not an obvious choice for princess moi (as Anne Lamott says), who abhors being wet and cold.

Matt insisted we could fix what was broken and create a refuge in and around the lush forest of oak and madrone trees, the ocean-drenched air, the view of Elephant Mountain. "Give it a try," he said. "If you don't like it, we'll move."

After a year of jumping over puddles in the kitchen, the living room, and the bedroom, and resenting my husband for his optimism, the second new roof stopped the inside rain. That left the other puddle: the swimming pool. For most buyers, it would have been an asset. For me, it was a liability.

My first memory of almost-swimming was standing at the edge of the Atlantic Ocean when I was two years old as my mother held my hands and dipped my toes in the waves. The unstoppable pull of the water terrified me, the way it dragged rocks and shells into its underneath. Where was it taking the shells? And would it take me, too? I kicked and thrashed and screamed until my mother carried me back to our navy blue plaid blanket on the hot, dry sand.

Thirty million years. That's how long it took for humans to crawl out of the sea and to grow arms and legs and lungs instead of fins and snouts and gills.

What's the rush to get back?

Water is where people drown, where boats are capsized, where sharks eat legs, arms, heads. The only time we kayaked, Matt and I, stranded and soaked, had to be rescued because our rudder broke. When I water-skied at camp, I couldn't stay upright. When I snorkeled, I couldn't stop breathing water. I am an earth creature. I like gravity. I like dirt. I like the crunch of a foot hitting the ground.

And please don't tell me what I already know: Seventy percent of the earth is water. Sixty percent of our bodies are water. Even our brains and bones are a third water. Honeybees and basil, poodles and petunias, salmon and seaweed depend on water for life. Without water, we humans die within eight days. I appreciate water, really I do. But I can do it without getting wet.

"Fill it with dirt," I said to the contractor that first year we lived in our cold damp house. "Let's get rid of the swimming pool and plant a garden instead."

"Live here for five years," he answered. "The summers are hot. Very hot. You might be grateful to have a pool to cool off."

Twenty-two sweltering summers passed without a thought of a toe in the pool. Even on ninety-degree days, I didn't want to be cold or wet. I kept waiting for the summer day I'd want to jump in, cool off, go swimming. It never came.

After the cancer diagnosis, my doctor suggested I take a three-minute cold shower every morning. I remember thinking that he was insane. That he didn't know me as well as I thought he did. That it was time to change doctors.

"No," I answered. "Absolutely not."

"Try it," he said. "It's okay to scream," he said. "Cold water is good for 'upregulating' the parasympathetic nervous system, increasing your energy, and decreasing inflammation. And it might make it harder for disease to proliferate in your body."

A cancer diagnosis bends the mind. It is terrifying, shocking. You suddenly realize that you will die someday. Those Buddhists weren't kidding. And you ask yourself what of your many fixed positions you are willing to reconsider.

The next morning, I stepped into the shower and turned the knob to cold. I screamed. Matt came running to ask if I was okay. "Fine," I said, through chattering teeth. I might have made it one minute that day. Maybe thirty seconds. But I did notice that when I stepped out of the shower, I felt invigorated, exhilarated, new.

"That's because you are no longer being thrashed by ice-cold water," Matt suggested when I told him about the exhilaration.

Maybe. But of the two—cancer or cold water—I chose cold water. The showers continued.

Then the physical therapist suggested that the bundles of nerves wrapped around the scar tissue in my breast that were causing so much pain might be stretched and relieved if I could walk in water and do breast exercises a few times a week.

I don't have water to walk in, I said. And then I remembered the body of it in my backyard.

The water is fifty degrees. I ask Matt to join me in the pool. He refuses. Then I ask if he will distract me from the freezing water by singing while I walk, swim, stretch. Yes, he says, he will do that.

When I first met Matt and I couldn't sleep, he would tell me silly stories about hands that grew toasters and girls who could fly on the backs of purple swans. No matter what he said, the rolling meadow of his voice always sounded to me like he was saying, "It's okay. Everything is okay." It still does.

He stands at the side of the pool in his hat, sweatshirt, polar fleece jacket, and down vest as I take one step into the water and scream. My skin feels as if it were being pelted by hail as big as houses. Then I realize it's easiest to just get it over with and submerge myself immediately. I take a deep breath, scream, say *"Oh my God,"* and start walking. Matt starts singing. (My favorites so far have been "Two Sleepy People" and "If I Were King of the Forest.")

Autumn becomes winter. Winter brings cold, rain, fog. Matt expands his repertoire to the Everly Brothers, Adele, Beyoncé. I watch his craggy face outlined by the silver slip of moon. His off-key voice, his Fats Waller accent, the way he pretends to be holding a mic, and drops out the *er*'s at the end of words (*better* is *bettah*, *forever* is *forevah*) make me momentarily glad to be doing this. To be doing anything anywhere that would fill the air with the sound of everything-is-okay.

Still. Every night, before I step into the water, I don't want to go. *I can't do this,* I think. There must be a better way to "upregulate" my immune system (and anyway, what kind of word is *upregulate?*). I feel like I am about to jump from a plane with no parachute. As if I were standing on a cliff about to splatter onto the rocks below. I've been in three almost-fatal car accidents and in the moments before the crash, when I saw the oncoming car, I wasn't afraid. But when I stand at the edge of the pool, I am afraid, convinced it's the end, I will die. No one ever accused me of not being melodramatic.

Until I touch the water, I am tired and dusty and grumpy from the day and I just want to get this over with, check "doing my best to deal with cancer" off the list. As I stand there dreading the next step down, I know who I am: a spouse, a daughter, a sister, a dog mother, a friend, a writer, a hummingbird lover. I know the answers to what I need to do tomorrow: Make the bed, meditate, walk with Matt, write, eat low-inflammatory food, make a plan for two future classes.

And then the cold meets my skin and my mind stops.

I look up at the sky. Up is down and down is up and I am swimming between stars, swinging my arms, tumbling like the rocks at the edge of the Atlantic Ocean into an underneath I can't see.

PART THREE

Leaving the Neighborhood

CHAPTER THIRTEEN

Girlfriends

Coco invites me into her small cottage, ambles toward me. Hugs me, kisses me on the cheek, motions for me to sit on the couch with her. I sit, cross my legs, bring out my phone, and press record on the voice memo app. She puts on a pair of black glasses. "Do those help you see?" I ask.

"No, but sometimes I can catch a glimpse of a color or shape on the periphery."

I don't think much about what it is like to be 90 percent blind, because Coco doesn't complain about it. At all. She says things like "I see less and less of the writing on my phone" or "I can't see anyone's face anymore" or "Will you look at the screen and tell me who is calling because Siri has decided to stay silent today." But she says it like I say that I wore a pair of flowered socks today. Simply and with no opinion.

When I sit with her, it is not just what she says that affects me, it is that I am entering a world in which everything is the way it is, without drama or desire for it to be different. I've never spent so many hours with someone who does not judge or complain, and that is as revolutionary to me as what she speaks about. When I sit with her, I watch her, feel her, and can't help but match her emanation of calmness, of everything is already fine except your belief that it isn't.

I tell her the story about my close friend Christine:

On the day I got my cancer diagnosis, I left a short message for my best friend, Christine, and asked her to call me.

When she called back, she cried. "Oh, sweetheart," she said, "this is just awful. But you will get through this, and Matt and I will be there each step of the way."

Christine and I had been friends for twenty years, since I asked her a question at a one-day workshop she taught.

"What about the abusive voice in my head that I can't silence or dispel?" I'd asked.

"So what?" she said. "That voice is like Gollum in the attic. Live downstairs where you can't hear him—and let him babble on and on all day, all night. Who cares what he shrieks about if you can't hear him?"

As soon as she said "So what?" I popped out of my skin like a genie from a lamp. Everything—chairs, the bald man next to me with phlegm in his throat, Christine's face—was made of a shimmer of pink-golden light. There were no edges, no boundaries, no rights or wrongs, no goods or bads, no differences between what was seeing and what was seen. The me that remained was in love with everyone, even the dentist, the cashier at the grocery store, and—the ultimate—the doctor who gave me a colonoscopy. It was a state of pure happiness. And it lasted six weeks, until fear pushed in and told me I was crazy, get real, come back to earth, little missy.

But in the meantime, and for the next twenty years, I ascribed the ability to transcend limitations and suffering to Christine, to her brilliance, to her spiritual mastery. And she'd chosen me as her best friend. I was smitten.

We talked a few times a week for an hour; we'd ramble on about everything from noninvasive face-lifts that weren't agonizing (Thermage, microneedling, laser resurfacing), where she wanted to live next (Nepal? Greece? Montana?), politics (what a shitshow), and feelings, always feelings. She described our talks as "beyond the space-time continuum, gliding in a palace of starlight." Afterward I felt bigger than and simultaneously more like me than before. When, ten or fifteen years ago, I told her that I was convinced I married the wrong man, she burst into laughter and knocked me back into what I knew that I forgot I knew. "Oh yeah," I said, "I can't imagine my life without Matt in it."

During our call about the breast cancer diagnosis, Christine reminded me that she hadn't had a mammogram in fifteen years—said the medical industrial complex was a sham—and floated the idea that the tumor might disappear, as many small cancers reportedly did, if I could watch it by getting a series of MRIs over the next few years. "There is a good chance you might not need a lumpectomy at all," she said. I liked that idea, being reluctant to become a cog in the wheel of the system—and the tumor *was* quite small. But I didn't have Christine's conviction and over the next few weeks, the onslaught of advice I received was "Remove the tumor *now*." Also, my friends were quick to point out that the four people we knew who decided on alternative treatment only died from the cancer they were certain that treatments like hyperbaric oxygen would cure.

A month after the surgery, when I told my oncologist that I didn't want radiation, which he and the surgeon and the gynecologist recommended, he became the teeniest bit hysterical. "You must! You must! You must get radiation! It will decrease your chances of recurrence from thirty percent to three percent." Another friend, every friend, agreed. Matt agreed. "What if there is just one cancer cell left after the surgery and it wanders and grows?" And so I decided on what seemed like the least invasive, least reprehensible radiation available, brachytherapy, which inserts radiation seeds directly into the tumor site through catheters and doesn't affect the lungs or the spine. Christine told me I was giving in, endangering my health, opting for a barbaric procedure.

On the day I left for the Arizona brachytherapy clinic, I felt like a wooden puppet, being moved from living room to car to airport, as if I were a character in someone else's nightmare. I called Christine on my way to the airport and she wanted to talk about breaking up with her current paramour and the new man, a well-known artist, she'd just met. "What do you think I should do?" I felt like she was talking to me from underwater and told her I was barely in my body, I couldn't discuss this now. She uttered a flattened "Okay" and got off the phone.

As the radiation flowed into my breast, I chanted, *I can live through this. I can resurface on Earth. There is light there. There is beauty there.* The overhead slideshow, which the clinic thoughtfully placed above the radiation table, flipped through landscapes and flowers and puppies with saucer eyes oozing cuteness. As the last slide, a meadow of tulips, flashed across the screen, I thought of the line from a Mary Oliver poem about poppies sending up their orange flares—right before the oncologist returned and said, "Done." He gave me a tiny wooden tiger, told me I was fierce.

When I got home, Christine didn't answer my emails or phone calls.

One day passed. Then another, then five days, a week. At first, I assumed she was busy. Then I decided my emails weren't being delivered. But after ten days of silence and twenty years of talking to her multiple times a week, I wondered if she was ending our friendship. I had watched her do this to other friends: stop returning phone calls, texts, and emails without explanation.

"They'll get the message," she'd say.

"But," I'd sputter, aghast. "Talk to them. Tell them how you feel. You've been close friends for thirty years."

"No point," she'd say. "I'm done with Lily/Abbey/Robert. And ending it without processing about it is clean."

Lily drank too much. Abbey left a bloodstained pillowcase in the guest room. Robert wouldn't lend her money.

This will never happen to me, I thought each time she ended a friendship. She told me I was her deathbed friend, asked me to be with her during her last few breaths. Surely she would never excise me from her life. I kept calling, emailing, concerned that she'd been in an accident or was ill.

Finally, after a silence of three weeks, she wrote, "Our friendship has been one-sided. It's not that you haven't been a good friend at times, but it's felt lopsided. I give to you and you don't reciprocate. It's best that we end this now."

I was sitting at my desk when I read those words. Once, twice, three times. She doesn't mean this. She *couldn't* mean this. She told me I was her deathbed friend! No. No. No.

And then the *what abouts* started:

What about the hours I spent with her agonizing about her first divorce, then her second and third? The money arguments, the living arrangements, the splitting up of art and furniture?

What about the seven thousand dollars I sent her two months before because she was low on money?

What about the days I spent putting flyers for her weekend retreat on lampposts and in grocery stores?

What about the love? The love. The love. The love. That unspoken connection—that trust that we saw each other, really saw each other, the messy, the brilliant, the crazy.

What about. What about. What about.

And you thought you'd gotten away with it, said Gollum who had moved into the living room—you thought you'd hidden yourself. Well guess what, sister, you've been found out.

I told no one, not even Matt, about the end of my relationship with Christine, because although he and I had been together for decades, I was convinced he'd suddenly realize our marriage was one-sided and that I was incapable of reciprocity. The shame began with Christine's withdrawal and deepened into the fact that I existed at all. I ricocheted from hearing Gollum in the living room tell me that I had always been a sham to chanting that I was selfish to the core to reminding myself that Christine was right, of course she was. You don't belong here, he'd snicker. You are damaged, better not let anyone know. And there it was: the same pattern, the same conclusions I'd come to with my mother: I was bad. I was selfish. I was unlovable.

The doctors called it radiation depression. They said some women weep every day for months after radiation as their bodies try to absorb the bombardment of photons. When I couldn't stop crying for eight months, I knew my depression was the shock of losing my best friend and the shame of believing I deserved it.

Occasionally, not often, I blamed Christine instead of myself: *Cancer! I had cancer! What kind of person ends a relationship during her friend's cancer treatment? What she did was savage, brutal, unconscionable. It is she that is damaged, not me.*

When, after a few months, I finally told close friends about Christine, they all, every single one, exploded. *Oh my God. Oh fuck. What kind of person does that? She is heartless. She's insane. Count yourself fortunate that she ended it.*

And there I remained: marinating in self-loathing while occasionally flipping to loathing Christine. As a child, I turned to frozen Milky Ways when I cried. Now it didn't occur to me to use food.

"It was brutal," I say to Coco as we sit on the couch. "She is heartless," I say.

I wait for Coco to be outraged about the situation. To murmur comforting words, to say, *Poor darling, that was vicious, unprovoked.* Instead she says, "Oh pooh." And then she asks, "What was the first lie you told yourself about her? Because that is when you started leaving yourself."

"Seriously?" I ask. "You're putting this on me?"

"Not on you," she says, "but it is *about* you." My head spins. She isn't buying the part about me being a victim and I hate her instantly.

She is turning this situation back to the lies I told myself, not to my jerk of a former best friend. But I am already marinating in shame, so I figure I have nothing to lose.

It takes less than a minute for me to realize I've been lying to myself about Christine for a few years by ignoring her actions and making excuses for her. By doing exactly what I did with my mother: blaming myself for her crazy behavior. Believing she was smart, beautiful, wise, and that I was selfish, wrong, damaged. The lie was that her behavior was an indictment of my value and not about her inability and unwillingness to reflect on her righteous and often preposterous behavior in which she was always right and the other was always wrong.

The time she stopped talking to me for a year because I gave a book she wrote to the head of Oprah's Book Club and not directly to Oprah herself.

The time she told me I'd plagiarized her work in *Women Food and God*.

The time her insurance company wanted to sue Matt and me because a limb fell on her car during the six months we'd allowed her to park on our property. "You will come to the courtroom if they sue me, won't you?" I asked. "Absolutely not," she answered.

The time I gave her a thousand dollars to hire a private detective when she was being stalked and she used the money for living expenses without telling me.

The times, so many times, she asked if I could help find a home for her books and, after hours of inquiry, I found two agents and a publisher who liked her work but unanimously agreed that it needed revision—and she refused, thought her writing was already perfect.

The times (every time) she insisted she was right about her every opinion and would not consider any other viewpoint.

The multiple times she asked friends for loans and they refused, citing her unstable financial situation. And how she called them wrong, greedy, selfish.

"The biggest lie," I tell Coco now, thinking of all of this, "is that I didn't see what I saw, feel what I felt. It is similar to when I confronted my mother about having affairs after hearing her on the phone with a lover and she insisted I was making it all up, that I didn't hear what I heard. And I chose to believe her, my mother, and tell myself I was wrong. I couldn't face the fact that my mother was a liar, a cheat.

"With Christine, I'd feel sick to my stomach, a low whisper that said, 'She's a little crazy, sweetheart, something isn't right in her psyche,' but I didn't want to face the consequences of knowing my best friend was slightly mad any more than I wanted to face that my mother was a liar and a cheat. I didn't want to be left alone. Except for breaking up with my college boyfriend who asked me to marry him, after which I dreamed of being in prison, I've never ended a relationship."

"So," Coco says, "you've been staying in a relationship that wasn't working and that you knew was over. You left it up to her to end what you wanted to end but didn't—and you were surprised?"

"Jeez, Coco," I say. "That's harsh. True, but harsh."

I feel like a dog that needs to shake herself out so I unfold my legs and walk to the bathroom, thinking, *Why exactly did I want to do this conclusion work? It is like lying in a bed of barbed wire.*

On the bathroom sink I notice a few skin products from Goop: eye depuffer pads, dark spot exfoliating lotion. I wonder how Coco can see well enough to locate the bags under her eyes, how she can even find her eyes. Maybe she can see more than she says she can see. Maybe she has been lying. Then I remember how she wobble-walks, reaches for walls to steady herself, can't find the buttons on her phone, and realize I am always suspicious. When the garbage-men don't pick up the trash, I'm certain they've forgotten our house. When I can't find my engagement ring, I'm certain it's been stolen. When I see depuffer pads, I'm certain Coco has been lying to me. I'm either about to be snookered or it has already happened. I might as well walk around with the back of my hand velcroed to the middle of my forehead sighing about being done wrong. Talk about seeing the world through the distortion of our wounds. The big exception, where I am continually snookered, is with girl-friends. In my relationships with women, I snooker myself.

When I settle myself back on Coco's couch I ask her how she locates the bags under her eyes for the depuffer pads and she says, "Oh, those aren't mine; my friend Yvette left them here. I could have steamer trunks under my eyes and not find them. But let's get back to Christine . . ."

Nailed again. I think but decide not to say *And I was afraid you'd been lying to me about being blind.* Instead I say, "Ending or leaving a relationship feels like saying, 'I'm fine the way I am.' Like closing the door to love, all love." I tell Coco, "If I turn down the chance, I will never get it again. I need to take what I can get."

"That unwillingness to leave is an effect but not the cause," Coco replies. "It's a reaction to a conclusion or belief about your-self. In this case (and likely with most women, beginning, I suspect, with your mother) it is the conclusion that you are unlovable. Have you noticed a pattern here, with other friendships?"

"My last best friend, Sharon," I offer reluctantly, "ended our friendship suddenly after sixteen years. My specialty seems to be getting involved with women whose specialties are sudden endings."

"They are mirroring your self-rejection," she says.

Oy. Again with "it's about me." I don't usually curse but with Coco, often, I feel like saying *fuck fuck fuck*.

"I *like* blaming," I tell Coco, and glare at her sitting peacefully on the couch. Once again, and for the thousandth time, I remind myself that she is blind and inured to looks that could kill. Her lower arms are sticking out of her flowered blouse. They wiggle, they hang, and, in this moment, I am smug about how much they sag. As if sagging arms mean anything about happiness. As if sagging arms cancel the truth she is offering. Make her less wise.

"So," she says, "how well has blaming worked with Christine? Because between blaming yourself and blaming her, it seems as if you are still actively suffering."

I know Coco is suggesting that I stop all blame and I can see quickly that this amnesty will include the white whale—my mother, the repository of a shitload of blame.

"Tell me more about Sharon." Before I open my mouth, I can see the lies and how I snookered myself. "Sharon was a well-known massage therapist in Buffalo. Beloved. Kind. After the very first day we met, we became fast friends. I allowed her to set the rules for our friendship—and she had many rules: meet once a week, talk every day, don't become friends with her friends."

I didn't realize then how much I rejected myself. How much I believed my conviction that I was unlovable, and that if an apparently kind woman like Sharon wanted me as a friend, I must agree to her rules so that I could bask in the reflected light of her love and be good by association. It will take another few years for me to realize that even when I "broke free from compulsive eating," even when I ate as much raw chocolate chip cookie dough as I thought I wanted, I still refused to allow myself what I really wanted, needed. I was still giving the power to determine my value to other people, in this case, my women friends.

As I work with Coco, I understand that since I was seeing myself through the distortion of the unlovable-wound, I was choosing friends who mirrored that wound back to me by how they treated me. It was as if I had a receptor site labeled "Unloved" and was unconsciously searching for someone to spark it. Like attracts like.

When I met Matt and moved to Berkeley, Sharon said that if I was moving, I needed to pay for that decision by being the one who drove to see her. Always.

If I bought Matt a computer, I needed to buy her one.

If I bought her daughter a sweater, I needed to buy her one as well.

Because she traveled to our wedding, I needed to travel to an art show of hers, when and if such a show was planned.

I was not supposed to see her acupuncturist or her massage therapist, or develop new friendships without her permission. I went along with it because I was too afraid not to. I didn't realize until now, working with Coco, how much I believed that I was damaged and the fact that Sharon loved me, wanted me, gave me worth.

Then, during a phone call, Sharon said, "I want you to dedicate your next book to me." I was standing in my kitchen, filling the kettle with water. I turned off the faucet. I stood, fixed in place. I thought, *She has to be kidding. She can't possibly demand a book dedication.* I looked out the window. The forsythia was blooming in bright gold. A finch hopped on one of its branches. I took a breath and said, "I love you but you cannot tell me who to dedicate my book to. That is not yours to decide."

"Why not? If I'm as important to you as you say I am, that deserves a book dedication. And by the way, please don't dedicate your upcoming workbook to me. I want you to dedicate a more important book than a workbook."

"No," I said. "You are always free to ask for what you want—and I know I haven't said many noes before—but no. This is up to me, not you."

When Sharon called a bookstore on the day my book *Appetites* was published and discovered that I'd dedicated it to Matt, she wrote me a short letter saying that she was ending our friendship.

Finally, Coco says, "You went to great lengths to keep from experiencing your self-rejection," to which I sigh loudly and say, "How about saying something about how friendships between women are tricky, that they have no rules like marriages or parental relationships? How about reflecting on the depth that women go to in their friendships and how painful it is when they end?" I am on a roll now, starting to pontificate about why women's friendships are an exception to her no-blame stance. "How about some compassion?"

"Compassion," she says, "is offering a way through the distorted lens of your conclusions about yourself. Because until you have named and forgiven yourself for believing what wasn't true, you will keep projecting your self-rejection out there and be shocked when it comes back to you in the form of rejection by others.

"So, tell me," she says, "the earliest memory you have of believing you were unlovable."

And here we go: back to childhood again. Coco is not influenced by my tirade and insistence that some people are brutal, mean, deserve to be blamed. During our work together, she has repeatedly brought me back to the conclusions a child makes about herself based on her environment. *My mother didn't pick me up at kindergarten* turns into *I was abandoned. My mother hit me* turns into *I am unlovable. My brother threw books at my head* turns into *I am a piece of shit.*

After weeks of working with Coco, I started calling the process the Unavoidable but Never True Conclusions I Made Before I Could Talk, and when I see how what I conclude about myself—*it's better if I don't exist, I can never get enough, I am dumb, I need too much, I'm a failure, joy is not for me*—gets projected on every single situation I encounter, I am flabbergasted. *A friend doesn't answer my text* turns into *I am unlovable.* Matt is late turns into *there's a catastrophe brewing.* I haven't written in a week turns into *I'm a failure.*

A few words about conclusions: They are the lens through which we see everything that matters to us and yet we are not aware of them at all. Why? Because when we first formed them, they were intolerable, almost unbearable—imagine a two- or three-year-old believing she is unlovable—so we covered them with shiny, socially sanctioned behaviors. We learned how to make our mommies laugh, how to be, perform, how to fit in, and we pushed the conclusions about being damaged or unlovable so far away that what remains of them is the belief that we are imposters in our own lives, since we know (but only vaguely) that how we appear or behave is covering up the messy, unspoken, and possibly intolerable beliefs about who we (believe we) actually are.

We live on top of ourselves by learning to control or stay away from situations that make us uncomfortable, that might trigger the intolerable glimmerings that we don't know how to name. We push down (i.e., repress) our conclusions and then we project them onto the people we know without understanding that all judgment is self-judgment. *She is mean. She is selfish. She is intolerable. She is fat.* We resent anyone who triggers our age-old conclusions, anyone who treats or talks to us in particular tones, and in that way, our lives get smaller and smaller. Or we walk around constantly triggered and in low-level fear, believing we are at risk and the world is on the verge of apocalypse.

Conclusions are painful to feel, name, and say out loud. But only at first. Then it's a relief to unearth what we know that we don't want to let ourselves know.

Most of us believe that we can't afford to be aware of the deepest deep, the darkest dark, as if awareness of what has been driving our behavior will destroy us. We are afraid that if we name it, we'll fall apart, won't take care of our kids, get to the bank, go to work. We've been brainwashed into believing that living on top of ourselves is living, when the opposite is true.

We will never be fully alive until we stop managing our lives and begin naming the lies—the never true but unavoidable conclusions—that are killing us slowly.

Being aware of them is the first step because when you throw the lights on, the dark disappears. It's a law of the universe.

Another reason that we don't name our conclusions about ourselves: We are convinced they are true. And when we believe they are true, it is excruciating to name them and say them out loud. I spent thirty years hiding the belief that I was inherently selfish from Matt. He had seen me bereft, anxious, depressed, judgmental, enraged, resentful, and yet I was still convinced that if he knew what my mother knew about me, he would be as disgusted as (I believed) she was and would leave me.

After being diagnosed with cancer, being ghosted by my best friend, I was in so much pain that I was willing to name the conclusions I'd avoided for almost seventy years.

Everyone has conclusions. Everyone, even those who had mothers by whom they felt adored, formed conclusions about their worth, their value, their lovability. Why? Because children are totally dependent on imperfect caretakers and even the most loving mother will forget, mess up, be lonely, sad, depressed, need to attend to herself first. The child interprets the lack of attunement to mean something is wrong with her and figures out how to behave to keep the love coming.

The whole system is a house of cards because it's built on one lie after another—starting with the belief that the mother's behavior is a reflection of the child's worth when, in reality, a mother's behavior is an expression of herself and her capacity at that moment. The conclusion the child makes is a creation, a total fabrication. And yet when she becomes an adult, she will continue to see through her fabricated conclusions for the rest of her life. She responds to situations, people, and her own feelings based on conclusions that were never true. And as if that weren't enough, those conclusions will be reflected back to her through the so-called external world. Whatever she believes about herself will return to her via friendships, lovers, colleagues, and she will be convinced that the external world is the cause, not the effect, of her feelings and beliefs.

My student Bebe is convinced she is unlovable. That she was born damaged, a bad seed. Her mother chased her around the kitchen with a butcher knife every day for a year beginning in first grade. "A mother doesn't do that for no reason," Bebe tells me.

She was in somatic and trauma therapy for ten years. Still, when we do the conclusion work, she says she is damaged and that is that. "You can't convince me otherwise."

I tell her she is right, that I can't convince her. That it is only by seeing that sweet little first grader running around the kitchen and naming the feelings and then the conclusions she came to that will dispel the unworthiness. When something—a conclusion—is installed at such an early age, it takes a fierce commitment to delete it. But, I tell her, you don't have to begin directly with your mother. You can start by naming what you believe about your friends. What triggers you, when you blame them, when you feel hurt.

Back to Coco, who after asking me to recall another memory of deciding I was unlovable, sits placidly. I almost always resist these suggestions because naming the memories that created the interpretations feels like being asked to chew a handful of nails. I squirm. I get up, walk around. Then I take a breath and flip through the Rolodex of unlovable memories, find the one marked "On the Train."

"My mother, brother, and I were on a train from San Antonio, where we'd visited my grandparents. We were cramped in a tiny cabin and when my mother slid the bathroom door open, I looked at her. I stared at her breasts. I hadn't seen her naked for a long time and her body fascinated me. When she saw me staring at her body, she got furious. 'You are always looking, aren't you? You are always staring, aren't you?'

"I wanted to be swallowed up, to disappear. I was so ashamed of looking, of wanting, of having hungry eyes."

"What kind of child," Coco asks, "would be yelled at for looking at her mother?"

"A child who was not supposed to exist. A bad child. An unlovable child."

"And when you see this, when you look at that child in the train compartment, can you turn to her in kindness and realize that the conclusion she came to was unavoidable but not true? Because until you name, feel, and forgive that original conclusion, you will be looking at the world through distorted lenses and acting surprised when the world looks distorted."

"Can we bring this back to Christine?" I say.

"We just did," she answers. "Everything you felt was you, only you."

"Fuck," I say.

CHAPTER FOURTEEN

The Six Steps

The chatter of the mynah birds in the monkeypod tree as I walk out of Coco's door is raucous, almost deafening. Chalk-white plumeria blossoms are strewn on the gravel path. It's the end of the day and the lemony spell of the sunset washes away the vestiges of agitation from the session with Coco.

I lean on the monkeypod trunk for a few minutes and wonder what the mynah birds are so busy talking about. Is it mating? Posturing? Their chatter sounds like a cross between singing and screaming: *That dove did me wrong. That cardinal took the food right out of my mouth. That damn nene cut me off. My best friend flew the coop and left me for another tree.* And the final squawk: *My mother gave more worms to the other fledglings; no wonder I take more than my share now.* Yup, I understand. It's hard to let go of being done wrong. The world as we know it is built on believing that they—whoever they are—are against us.

I think about Christine as I walk to the car. And Sharon, my best friend before her. And Polly, my one romantic female relationship that was even more disastrous than those without sex. Polly broke up with me by disappearing for a week. When I went to her house, frantic that she was lying dead on the floor, I rifled through her trash and read a letter to her therapist—with whom she had just started a clandestine relationship—in which she, Polly, called me neurotic, needy, and fat. I was crushed.

What a mess, I think, as I climb into the hot car, turn on the engine. I used to think that my friendships with women were stellar, that women knew how to be more sensitive, aware, relational than men. But I'm realizing now that it doesn't matter if it's a woman, a man, a dog, a bird; if I am seeing them through the distorted lens of a wound, everything I see will be distorted. I can complain, try to fix someone else, ask them to treat me differently, but I will never be any saner than my conclusions.

And if that isn't bad enough, blame and righteous indignation have no place in this process—a fact about which I am righteously indignant. When your mother beats you, when your best friend ends your relationship on the day you return from radiation, when your lover breaks up with you without telling you, why shouldn't you be indignant? I wear my wounds like I wear my 1969 Rudi Gernreich saffron-and-red-checkered dress that has molded to my body's curves and lines. After all these years, it feels like me.

The "meta" voice, the noticer—true nature, presence, or what Ram Dass called loving awareness—answers simply that "blame hurts." It's the old saying, attributed to any number of sources but likely originating in Alcoholics Anonymous in 1935, about drinking rat poison and waiting for the rat to die. I am so used to drinking rat poison and then wailing and writing about having drunk rat poison that I don't know what will be left of me if I stop. If I don't wrap myself around being the abused daughter of a self-absorbed mother, if I don't parade around in being special because I was so abused, who is left?

I am thinking of one of my students whose mother brandished a gun and threatened to kill her when she came home late from school. In the ten years I've been working with her, there hasn't been a session in which mother, gun, chase wasn't mentioned. My student is seventy-nine and has been wearing the mother-daughter-gun mantle for so long that when I ask her to imagine who she would be without it, she replies, "I'd be invisible. I'd disappear." She keeps saying she wants to let her wounds go, but it seems as if she wants to keep them close more than she wants to let them go. Me too.

I was drawn to Coco for the same reasons I was drawn to Buddhism, the Diamond Approach, Internal Family Systems, Somatic Experiencing: to unwind the self-hatred that was coiled like a cobra around my heart. And to know myself as the loving awareness that Ram Dass promised was possible. To live wide-awake instead of walking around in a glaze of ongoing *no, this isn't it, I never get it right.* To be happy just because.

The process Coco teaches is called the Six Steps to Freedom and was created by Diederik Wolsak. Diederik adapted them from *A Course in Miracles,* and Coco further adapted them to include what she calls awake awareness or true nature. And because I have now been working with these steps for five years, I've adapted them further and added my understanding of the process as well as the places I've stumbled, resisted, and, eventually, surrendered.

STEP ONE: RECOGNIZE THAT YOU ARE TRIGGERED

The first step is to acknowledge the upset, which means recognizing that something has happened and that your response is to be triggered or charged, which often manifests as a physical sensation. Your stomach might contract, your heart might pound, your back might ache, your throat might close. We often override this step by normalizing it with a shrug and saying, "Well, who wouldn't be upset?" or "Of course I'm upset. That person left me/lied to me/excluded me."

It took months—I'm a slow learner—for me to realize that my response/trigger comes from my personal history and is not about the event or situation.

Matt doesn't get upset when he is not invited to a friend's gathering. I do.

My friend Jane isn't triggered by unanswered texts, emails, and phone calls. I am.

My brother doesn't react when my mother talks to him in her spiky voice. I do.

My response to the trigger is directly related to my conclusion, about which I am often unaware until I take myself through the rest of the steps.

This step may seem obvious—pounding heart, churning stomach, reddened face—but realizing you are triggered is subtler than it sounds because it seems obvious that the situation and person that catalyzed the trigger are to blame. When Christine ended our relationship, I blamed her for the devastation that followed rather than questioning the source of the shame; it was like looking in a mirror, seeing that my hair was a mess, and deciding to clean the mirror instead of brushing my hair.

STEP TWO: IT'S ABOUT ME

For the first four years I worked with these steps, I was like a donkey trying to throw "it's about me" off my back.

"Nope," I'd say. "Not this time. It sounds good," I'd say, "but this time, it's about Christine. If she had treated me kindly, I wouldn't be upset. So therefore, it's about her not me."

I balked and brayed about this step. I hated turning the upset around to me. I really, *really* wanted it to be about her/him/them. I wanted to blame, to get the whole mess out of my mind by believing that I wouldn't be feeling any of it if she/he/they hadn't done the dirty deed. I've died a thousand deaths on the sword of this step. Finally, most of the time, I accepted that change was possible only when I turned my outward-facing gaze to the cause of the wound— my own beliefs and conclusions. Which does not mean that I am happy about it, only that I know it's the truth.

"It's about me" is counter to every impulse, every principle we learned about communication in relationships, every bit of information we read in the news—all of which either directly state or imply that the other people are to blame and that the solution is on the level of the problem—by fixing what is apparently wrong. If we can just get our partner to agree with us, if we can just get our boss to stop criticizing us, if we can just eat or exercise enough to flatten our belly or find the correct skin cream to erase the lines on our face, if we could just kick this president out of office, we'd feel better, be better. This step is where righteous indignation falls apart like a tattered dress.

Slowly, ever so slowly, I understood that I have a basket of conclusions about value, self-worth, having and being enough, that is always there, running like an operating system in the background. Even if Christine and I were still friends, this conclusion would be waiting in the wings for the next triggering event.

Without my conclusions, I might have felt surprised, shocked, even heartbroken by Christine's withdrawal, but I wouldn't have felt ashamed that she was seeing the truth of who I'd always been that I'd kept hidden from my husband of multiple decades.

STEP THREE: NAME THE FEELING

Most of us are practiced at *thinking* our feelings, at reacting to or from our feelings because we have an idea that feeling our feelings means being consumed by them. But feelings are still there, whether we name them or not. And we're reacting to them whether or not we name them. If we're feeling angry or betrayed or lost or deficient and we don't name the feeling, everything we do and say is colored by it. When you name the feeling, you are able to witness it with awareness rather than merging with it and getting swept away by it. You realize that you *have* a feeling instead of believing you *are* the feeling. It's the difference—and I know this is a leap—between having a coffee cup and being a coffee cup.

STEP FOUR: REMEMBER THE FIRST TIME YOU FELT THIS

This is another one of the steps I resist. Back to childhood? Again? Do I have to? Why should I? Haven't I had enough therapy, hit enough pillows? If those things had worked, I'd be healed now. No thank you. Not going there again . . .

But going back allows me to see myself as I was. The first time it happened, I was so busy reacting to it that I didn't actually feel it. I pushed the confusion or rage or rejection away, and I adapted behaviors—being tough, being bossy, being obstinate—that allowed me to survive. This, and the next step, are the ones that allow me to melt the resistance I have to that chubby, crooked-banged girl. To feel what she felt. To be kind.

STEP FIVE: WHAT YOU CONCLUDED ABOUT YOURSELF THEN

When your mother left, when your father hit you, when you were bullied or put on a diet, what did you believe this meant about you? What kind of child deserves to be hit or left? What kind of child has the food taken out of her mouth by her mother? Is put on a diet by her mother at age eleven?

THE SIXTH STEP: FORGIVENESS

I've never liked the word *forgiveness,* because I thought it meant condoning reprehensible behavior. Also, I built an identity on holding grudges, on saying no. My mother told me once that "you can forgive and forget, but never forget that you've forgiven."

When my parents wouldn't admit that anything was wrong, when my father laughed when I told him my mother said they were getting a divorce, when my mother lied to me about her affairs with men, when she complained about what an awful lover my father was, I stopped asking them to acknowledge that something was wrong. I stopped pointing to the proverbial elephant and became her. They wouldn't admit to the elephant so I became one. I became the naysayer, the holder of grudges, the one who wouldn't let anyone pretend that we were a happy family, the one who wouldn't let anything go. I turned sullen, morose, prickly.

I hear the word *forgiveness* and think: *I'm supposed to forgive my mother for being an abusive, neglectful parent? Forget it*. But according to the Six Steps, I am not forgiving her for hitting me, lying to me, criticizing my body. I am not condoning what she did. I am forgiving myself for believing that what she did meant I was reprehensible.

When (in chapter four) my mother called me fat, I stomped around in old injuries, was outraged, blamed her.

HERE IS A REDO OF THAT SITUATION USING THE STEPS.

1. The trigger: My mother called me fat. How do I know I was triggered? I was furious, felt sorry for myself, compared myself to Charles Manson.

2. It's about me. When my mother called me fat, I'd just walked in from a beautiful morning with my retreat group. I was calm, peaceful. And then she called me fat and I was no longer calm or peaceful, so why wasn't my lack of peace about her? Because it was happening in my mind, my body. Because it was about where her words landed in me, about what it triggered in me.

3. The feeling that her words elicited in me: Outrage. Hurt. Shock. Humiliation.

4. A memory of the first time (or one of the first times) I felt those feelings. As I ask myself about an early memory of feeling humiliated, I remember something I have never remembered or

talked about: I am eight years old, standing next to the banister of our Jackson Heights house. I can see the cherry-colored rug and the lush velvet couch in the corner. My mother is furious. Her face is flushed. She is panting as she comes toward me with a stick. I back up, try to run up the stairs. She catches me and cracks the stick on my legs, my arms. I scream, then cry. She sends me to my room. She has hit me only with her hands before, not a stick, and I can see the welts now on my legs and arms.

5. My conclusion. I am not immediately certain what it was, so I ask myself: What kind of child would a mother hit with a stick? I go back, back, back to the red carpet, the velvet couch, my mother's face, the splinters on the stick. I feel myself standing there, terrified. A child, I answer, who was so bad she deserved to be beaten. An irredeemable child.

6. In Diederik Wolsak's version of forgiveness, I am supposed to say: "I forgive myself for ever believing I was bad. It could never be true." But when I do that, I feel as if I were repeating lines of a poem I was supposed to memorize.

Instead, I continue with feeling that child, her humiliation, her shame at being herself. And as soon as I see her, feel her with this kind of attention and clear-eyed awareness, my heart opens, swells, shatters into a thousand pieces. I don't flinch from the shattering—a broken heart, I remind myself, can hold the universe—and I know that what I concluded is not true. It was never true. That girl, with the crooked bangs and the black pedal pushers, adored her mother. That girl would have turned herself into a field of daisies for her mother to walk on. She would have lain in front of her mother for more slaps, more sticks, if it would have made her mother happy. That girl was doing the best she knew to do. I can feel the tears dripping down her cheeks. And I know that the conclusion about her was never true.

The eyes that see her are not my day-to-day eyes. I am not looking from my personality, my history. The perspective is from a higher dimension, presence itself. What Coco calls awake awareness. What Ram Dass called loving awareness. It is clear, bright, unaffected by opinions or circumstances. It is always there, always free, the eyes behind my eyes. Behind everyone's eyes.

It seems that the distance between being happy and being miserable is made of the lies we tell ourselves. And the way to see through our mind-made conclusions is to name and question them, beginning with the awareness that we are making them up. The Six Steps are not the only way to dissolve wounded conclusions, but they are the most direct and effective way I've found.

Sometimes a conclusion will need to be revisited tens of times (see the next chapter, "And Then, Forgiveness"). We've been living with and as that conclusion for decades without questioning it or realizing there is another way. It takes patience to keep questioning the lies we've told ourselves. But what else do we have to do besides dissolving what keeps us miserable and small and ashamed?

CHAPTER FIFTEEN

And Then, Forgiveness

A week passes. I am walking up the steps to Coco's cottage, ready to tell her that some people are so brutal they deserve blame.

"Tell me again what you mean by forgiveness," I say to Coco, "because I don't seem to be getting it. . . ."

"Forgiveness," Coco responds, "is the act of seeing the conclusions with awareness because when you do, you also see that your interpretations are based on a limited version of what happened."

"Even if your mother dragged you across the floor by your hair?" I ask. "If she told you that you were born damaged?"

"Yes. I'm not saying that wasn't painful. But what matters now is what you still believe about the kind of person you were—and still are."

This is about the fourth or fifth conversation we've had about forgiveness and it still hasn't clicked. I feel as if she is speaking gibberish. New Age blather. I don't like having this thing turned on me. I was a child, for God's sake.

"It is seeing that your conclusions about being selfish or worthless were unavoidable. But they were never, not for one minute, true. Yes, your mother told you that you were selfish, but then you created an identity based on that and you kept embroidering it over the years so that when anything didn't go the way you hoped or expected it would, you blamed yourself. You say things like: No wonder no one talked to me at the party. No wonder Jesse didn't answer my call. No wonder I didn't get invited to that girls' weekend. *I'm selfish. I'm damaged. Of course that happened.*"

I hate this line of thinking and now I hate Coco, her fat ankles, her stringy hair, her lopsided walk.

A few weeks later, when I am back in California, Coco and I are still having the blame conversation during our calls. I can't quite buy what Coco is saying: that my mother did what she did and that I created/made up a story of what that meant about me, a story I am still believing. That I now see myself through the story, through conclusions about myself that I *made up*, which were unavoidable but never true. That I see the world through wounded eyes and that, therefore, I see wounds where there are none.

When a friend doesn't answer my call for a few days, I devolve into what I believe it means about me. I eliminate the possibilities that she is sick, away, busy, and turn them into the conclusion that I am unlovable, am irrelevant, don't matter. I am like the spectators on the basketball court in the experiment of a man dressed in a gorilla costume marching across the court while the people watching the game were so focused on the players, they could not, did not, see him.

I am so focused on seeing the world as my wounds are that I don't see what is not wounded. Coco insists there is no objective or concrete "out there" out there, that I see what I believe. Except that when I write or teach, the me that gets triggered, that takes things personally, disappears—and in its place is what psychologist Mihaly Csikszentmihalyi labeled the flow state. Total absorption. Utter enjoyment. Seeing the sun rise. Walking in the forest. Meditating. Making love. Cooking a meal. Creating art. The whole point of doing the conclusion work is to see past the identity we've created from our wounds, to dispel the me-person we believe we are—and to be happy. To live with a fundamental ease of being that is our true nature. Without our conclusions, we would all live in a flow state.

"I suppose it's lucky," I tell Coco, "that I spend hours, days, weeks writing and teaching, during which, thank you, God, my mind stops and something beyond this everyday wounded self comes through and I know what I didn't know I knew until that moment. I feel exalted, relieved of conclusions and suffering, until, alas, I clunk back into my familiar historical self."

"So, you already know what it's like to dispel the conclusions and rest in the truth of who you are, who you have always been: the awareness that's never been touched by your past. . . ."

"Don't take this too far," I say. "I'm not used to calling myself lucky. I feel like I'm going to get in trouble for saying it out loud. It's much more comfortable to see myself as wounded."

"And now we're back to the conclusions," Coco says. "On some level there was an 'out there' out there. Something happened. Your mother hit you, neglected you, lied to you, and you concluded that the kind of girl those things happen to must be worthless, irrelevant. And from those conclusions, you developed a set of adaptive behaviors—being nice, being generous when you didn't feel like it, pushing your anger down, saying yes when you meant no, mistrusting yourself—to get the love you believed you could have if only you were not who you believed you were."

I am still not convinced by what she is saying. And I am starting to get distracted. The dishes are piled up in the sink. The trails of egg yolk on the plate are hardening. I have emails to write, calls to return. I'm tired of talking about forgiveness. I want to wash the dishes and get back to it.

"Stop for a moment and consider the amount of hatred you have heaped on that kid. And begin forgiving yourself for how you treated her/yourself because of believing what was never true."

My mother recently told me that she didn't drag me by my hair. "I might have yanked the littlest bit," she says, "but I definitely did not pull you across the floor."

And yet I remember the pull, the drag, the pain. I've recounted it so many times that it picks up bits of drama and detail every time I say it. The brown-and-black wallpaper in the hall. The sound of my feet dragging on the tile floor. The brass umbrella stand in the shape of a giant boot. Did it happen the way I remember it? Or the way it needs to have happened for me to keep blaming her? Blame, it seems, depends on believing that *the way* I saw what happened is what happened and not a subjective interpretation of it.

If she did drag me across the floor, which, at this point, I am unsure about, it happened once. Then, and until now, I have dragged myself across the floor hundreds of times by recounting it, remembering it, blaming her for it. Do I forgive myself for the meaning I gave to those hundreds of times? Because what I concluded those memories meant about me was that I was so bad I deserved to be slapped, dragged, screamed at.

But even as I describe the feeling of being trapped in a corner, my mother's hands grabbing my hair, I think: *I've been telling the same stories for years with the same inflections.* It's as if I were reading from a dog-eared script: "Can you ba-leeve the mother I had?" In this sunburned-story, the voice is sad, becomes syrupy, turns indignant, and ends in a last gasp of pitiful.

I recognize this recitation. My friend Marie told her troubadour-in-Europe story with the same inflections whenever we'd meet someone new: singing "Like a Rolling Stone" on the streets of Amsterdam, running out of money in Paris, hitchhiking to Barcelona. It was as if she-now was hovering to one side while performing the lines she'd memorized of she-then.

I am getting bored by my own stories but I don't know what will replace them. Also, I don't want to let my mother off the hook.

Years ago, I read an article about forgiveness and apologies. It said that for an apology to be successful, three elements needed to be included: the apologizer needed to be convincing about being sorry; she has to say she will never do it again; and she must make a meaningful offering (flowers? chocolate? her firstborn child?). I've used those steps with my husband many times, especially the flowers part. But as I think of them now, I realize that wanting an apology assumes that I am hurt or angry because someone did something offensive and not because of the meaning I gave to it. It puts the blame on the apologizer and leaves me with the same beliefs, interpretations, meanings ready to pop up with the next trigger, the next offense. (Being an adult is not as much fun as I thought it would be.)

A year ago, a colleague indignantly told me that I'd been neglecting the eighth eating guideline I'd written. "Why aren't you teaching that?" she asked. For a moment I thought, *I can't believe how irresponsible I am. What is wrong with me?* And then I remembered—it took longer than you'd expect—that there are only seven guidelines, that it was I who wrote them and my colleague was wrong. Even without a long-held conclusion being restimulated, the predisposition to doubt myself is noteworthy.

Coco says, "This is only about you."

But. But. But. "Even if I forgive myself, that still leaves the resentment toward her."

"You're making a category error," Coco says. "You believe, along with most of the eight billion people on the planet, in cause and effect. Your mother's behavior was the cause and your self-hatred is the effect. But if that were true, your brother would have the same tendencies to turn on himself, and from what you have told me, his confidence belies that."

Cause and effect are mistakes? My mother's behavior did not cause (the effect of) my conclusions about myself? One thing doesn't lead directly to another?

I remove my attention from the hardened egg yolk and try to understand what Coco is saying; she often comes out with things that flip what I think I know into a dimension I never knew existed and simultaneously recognize as a truth I've forgotten about. Then I remember what Nietzsche said: "There are no facts, only interpretations." And I remember what Gabor Maté said: that it's not what happened, it's what we believed or internalized about what happened, that causes the pain. It's not that my mother hit me, it's what I concluded about myself when she hit me that is so painful. The world turns on this understanding that it's not what happened, it's how I interpreted what happened because it puts a full stop to being a victim of circumstances beyond our control (the cause) and allows us to be in control of the interpretations we make (the effect) from those circumstances.

We see what we believe. All we ever experience "out there" is who we are being to ourselves "in here." We are our own creations. That's it. That's all.

Etty Hillesum was twenty-nine years old when she was deported to Auschwitz. A horrendous, tragic situation, and yet she is reported to have thrown flowers from the train to Auschwitz, and a postcard written in Hillesum's handwriting and found by a stranger read: "*We left the camp singing.*" It is almost impossible to believe that she threw flowers, sang, and maintained a loving perspective while riding in a cattle car to her death. But if we see what we believe and if there are "no facts, only interpretations," then we need to assume that benevolence is possible anywhere, anytime. And that Etty Hillesum knew that. Became that. And—I say this to myself often—if one person can do it, be it, become it, anyone can. I can. You can. Anything is possible.

CHAPTER SIXTEEN

Choosing My Mother

Three spiritual teachers and a writing mentor told me that we choose our mothers because of what we learn by being with them. I used to think that meant I was a masochist. But now a muffled voice says, "Without her, you never would have struggled with food, written books, gone to India, learned to meditate, decided to work with Coco."

"I don't think you chose this person, this mother, per se," a leathery-faced teacher in Bali once told me, "but it might be true that you had a soul plan, and having this mother was a way to learn what you came here to learn."

For some reason, and although the words *soul plan* sounded like more New Age blather, I understood this. Not with my mind, but with a knowing that does not need verification or validation from somewhere or someone else. Because beneath all the stories of what she did, I *recognize* my mother: the timbre of her voice, the raising of her eyebrows when she emphasizes certain words, the dips of her laughs. The sound of her sighs. Her sassiness. Her wit. Her judgments. Knowing her is like being inside a song that has been playing since before I was born.

If I let go of what author Caroline Myss calls woundology (cleaving to my abuse story), my mother is not right, wrong, good, bad. She is the way she is. Was the way she was.

I can't point to a beginning; what happened between us occurred long before she became a mother. Was it that she felt hated by her own mother? Was it after her cousin Sandy put his hands on her breasts when she was ten? Coming home from school to an empty house and eating loaves of challah slathered with butter to assuage her loneliness? Being called fat by her sister, mother, father? Does it go back further to my great-grandmother who escaped Russian pogroms and for whom mothering did not include physical affection and talking about feelings? If there are undisputable facts, they are these: An unmothered daughter becomes a mother in a loveless marriage at age twenty-two and the overeating and the unmothering and the body-self-hatred continue.

Without the assignation of cause (i.e., the beginning) and effect (the consequence of that beginning) there is nothing to point to and say "It started here."

It is the middle of the night. I wake up to the sound of the frogs ribbiting in the small concrete pond outside the back door. I look around. I blink in the darkness and it is then that I hear my mother's voice calling me.

"Genie," she says. "Genie," she says again, "look at me."

I think of the lines from the movie *David and Lisa* when Lisa says, "David, David, look at me, who do you see, who do you see?" and he answers, "I see a girl, who looks like a pearl. A pearl of a girl." In that half-sleeping, half-starry state, I can see my mother's face and I see a girl, a pearl of a girl.

I see her as she was at ten years old walking down a Bronx street with her grandfather David on Sunday afternoons. He is wearing a dark brown pin-striped suit, brown scuffed shoes, has a long white beard and huge hands. I see my one-day mother stopping to croon at every dog that prances by, hear her grandfather cluck and tell her that she has the soul of a dog.

I see her sledding down Spinney Hill in Queens when she was eighteen, her hair curly from the Toni Home Permanent she just gave herself, her cheeks flushed and expectant.

"Genie, Genie, look at me, who do you see, who do you see?"

I see a girl, Mom, a pearl of a girl. I see you before you were a mother.

I see the moon in your eyes, the sliver of hope for love you didn't feel as a child.

I see that you believed you were fat and decided to marry the first man you kissed, my father, and I see your loneliness when he left in the mornings and didn't come home until late at night.

I hear you singing "Que Sera, Sera" to me, your voice like a drift of clouds surrounding us.

I see that you wanted children but were so young that you were still a child yourself.

I see that you treated us the way you treated yourself. And that there wasn't anything else you could have done. I see the pearl of a girl you were, Mom, and that you still are.

I have defined myself for so long within the context of my relationship with my mother—my eating was in response to her, my feelings about my body, about my value—that when that disappears, the me that was created from my interpretations, the ego itself, disappears as well.

When I wake up in the mornings after my middle-of-the-night visitations from my mother, I throw off the covers, slip out to the courtyard to take a walk, clomping on the antique limestone pavers in the living room. The irregular swirls of gold and terra-cotta on the pavers make me happy whenever I take the time to notice them. The person we bought them from told us they were saved from the streets of old Jerusalem, and when I told that to Rafael, the man who set them, he said, "I bet Jesus walked on them!" Then, when other workers arrived to help him, he'd exclaim that "Jesus walked here."

I reach for the handle on the front door and hear my mother's voice again. "Genie," she says, "look at me. Look at me. Who do you see?"

I look again—this time with a time-lapse camera at the hair-dragging incident—and I see two people, a big person and a small one, engaged in what looks like a struggle. I move the camera to the right and see a tile floor with specks of gold and taupe. I keep moving the camera and see the bigger person yanking the smaller person's hair. I look at the big person's face and see a child in an adult body who couldn't give what she'd never received.

I'm crunching on a gravel path now, walking fast, passing a row of succulents leading to a jade tree in a large cobalt-blue planter.

Forgiveness might be acknowledging the way my mother and

I meshed—the way her rejecting behavior matched my vulnerability to being rejected—and honoring the process of emerging from the host of conclusions. Honoring that which was never vulnerable, never hurt, never stained, but which, it seems, I know only by working through the feelings and beliefs that keep me from knowing that unobstructed ease of being.

The driveway outside our gate leads up a steep hill to a longer driveway down to the mailbox. *Might as well go up the hill,* I think, maybe I can walk faster than my mind can think. I see myself at eight, nine, ten: the chubby legs, the crooked bangs, the longing for the blond goddess-mother who turned heads wherever we went. How that child turned to frozen Milky Ways for comfort. And I watch the immediate revulsion that comes up when I remember her chubby legs, her desperate wanting. How vehemently I turned my mother's neglect onto myself, coiled it into fierce self-hatred. Now, without resistance to feeling the bewilderment of that child, tenderness appears.

It is, I recognize, the sweetness of forgiving the years of rejecting and abandoning myself.

I'm remembering what I heard Byron Katie say: that forgiveness is realizing that what you thought happened never happened. Without my conclusions of being unlovable, unwantable, my friend Christine's withdrawal would have been mystifying but not shattering, because I would have realized this was her ongoing pattern. It was not about me. Just pondering this makes me feel disoriented, as if I have spaghetti coming out of my ears.

By forgiving myself, I also, inadvertently, forgive Christine. If I'm not shocked, hurt, betrayed, affronted (which does not mean I am not affected by the loss), if I don't think that her behavior is because of my, or her, deficiency—it simply is what it is. I inch toward forgiving my mother or at least tell the truth that trying to punish her for half a century hasn't yielded positive results.

Who will I be if I'm not blaming myself or someone else?

Free, I think, *I will be free.* Because when I drop the conclusions, I already am. When I stop playing the movie of my childhood, what is left is without drama.

At some point, it becomes a choice to use the triggers to remind me that below the shame of being rejected is a conclusion that child made because she had no other choice at the time. I can keep constellating around the child or recognize the triggers—feeling rejected, abandoned; being tired, lonely—that send me into believing the conclusions. Or I can use them as doorways into what waits like a prayer for my attention.

Perhaps the spiritual life (and if you can think of a better word than *spiritual,* please let me know) is about what I see, feel, know when I stop playing the movie and remove the distorted lens through which I see it.

A footstep scrunching on gravel. A drift of forget-me-nots popping up in the meadow. My best friend ending our relationship. Being diagnosed with cancer. My husband's craggy face. A smattering of stars. The ongoing pain in my breast. The explosion of cherry hazelnut chocolate on the tongue. The crack of a tree falling. And swimming in the sky.

CHAPTER SEVENTEEN

Drunk on Gardenia

I'm sitting outside at a dinner party with ten people on a balmy full-moon September evening. I'm staring up at the harvest moon, which is supposed to offer grounding, abundance, and all-around sanity, trying to remember lines from Dorianne Laux's poem "Facts About the Moon" so I don't strangle the hostess.

> *. . . We don't deserve the moon.*
> *Maybe we once did but not now*
> *after all we've done.*

It's seven thirty. The party started at six p.m. and, except for a handful of corn chips and a ho-hum hummus spread, no food has been served. Five people around me say "I'm hungry, when will the food arrive?" but then, maddeningly, they continue sitting with legs crossed, burbling to the person next to them. Only I, it seems, am harboring an inner Draymond Green, the Golden State Warriors forward who has stomped on, choked, punched, and almost knocked out opponents who have angered him. Until tonight, I've been disgusted with his outbursts—"Keep it together, Draymond!" I've yelled at the television screen—but he is my hero now as civility and impulse control are waning and my desire to stomp on the hostess's head gains traction. A few more lines from Laux's poem scrawl across my mind:

What bothers me most is that someday
the moon will spiral right out of orbit
and all land-based life will die.

Laux is one of my favorite poets—her language is simultaneously exultant and personal—and this is one of my favorite poems, but then I think: *To hell with orbits and death.* What bothers me most is not the damn moon or even the death of countless species, humans included, but that Rose, the hostess, is nonchalantly, as if we weren't here, talking to Max, her husband.

She finally moves into the kitchen. She can't decide whether to put the food indoors on a buffet table or outdoors, and I say, perhaps too forcefully, "Put it anywhere, just put it!" I take the dishes out of the oven, the microwave, the refrigerator. She asks the guests to form a circle, says a blessing to thank everyone for coming, and then goes on to thank the earth, the rain, the people who grew the rice, picked the vegetables, delivered it all (Will she also thank the steering wheels, the brake pedals, the washing machines that cleaned the clothes of the truck drivers?), and then, finally, it's time to eat. I scoop curried fish and roasted broccoli onto my plate, go outside, remind myself to slow down, to taste the food for which I've been waiting forever—and little by little, I calm down. Upon finishing the last bite, I consider my descent into almost-madness, as if I'd woken from a drunken stupor and were looking around to see where I dropped my clothes. I have a hangover—muted shock and amazement—from my violent inclinations and I decide it is best to remove myself to Rose's backyard, as I am certain that saying "So, did you want to kill Rose, too?" is not engaging party talk.

The gardenia bushes in the garden where I now walk fill the air with a creamy, peachy fragrance so enveloping, so heavenly, that it makes me want to dive into them and disappear. I smile and think that, well, disappearing into a bush would be a convenient way to avoid reckoning with wanting to pummel Rose.

I don't know where to start the inner questioning since my reaction to a delayed dinner was rather extreme.

I no longer have low blood sugar, so wanting to punch the hostess did not come only from hunger.

I don't usually like parties, but there was so much about being at this one that was loveliness itself: looking at the saucer moon, listening to the rustling of the wind through the trees, hearing the murmurings of people talking, presenting Rose with multiple bouquets of orchids and roses and tuberose.

It's clear, I realize, that even after decades of writing and teaching about compulsive eating, I still have a "food issue." Not a weight issue, not a stop-when-you're-full issue, not a which-food-shall-I-eat issue, not an overeating issue—a food issue.

Food was my best friend during the seventeen years I ricocheted up and down the scale. It was always there. It was always comforting. It always tasted good. It didn't talk back. It didn't go away. It didn't hit or yell or lie. One of my teachers said, "You never divorce anyone. The imprints of a relationship live inside you forevermore." Same, it seems, with the relationship with food:

I still eat before I eat. A corner of cheese. Crumbs of crackers, wedges of sweet potatoes, spoonfuls of sauces, as if I have to eat it before I'm not allowed to eat.

I still eat for the hunger to come by eating slightly more than enough.

I still eat quickly, almost furtively, as if my mother will catch me and I'll get in trouble.

I still act as if I were stealing food, as if I was not supposed to receive pleasure from what was previously forbidden.

I still prefer sweet foods over any other, a habitual response to being told I was not allowed to eat them.

I still eat chocolate twice a day to say fuck you to everyone who told me I was allergic to it.

And although I know that these behaviors are a reaction to what I was told I should or shouldn't do as a child, I notice now that I don't care. Without judgments, there's no suffering, no fight, no story, no good or bad. Eventually the patterns will do what all patterns do when they aren't resisted: die of neglect like a once-used path in the forest now covered with moss and scattered leaves. And if they don't disappear, if they sing their food songs for the rest of my life, it's fine with me—and this, of course, is a triumph. I spent most of my life resisting, fighting, and being convinced that these patterns needed to disappear for me to be happy. Now I just notice them.

In the dappled light of the harvest moon I realize once again that food issues are life issues. Any issue about food threads through everything—every nonedible relationship, every situation. How you eat is how you live.

The opening notes of the happy birthday song are floating into the garden now as I circle the stone path, once, twice, listening to the chorus of voices. The party is coming to a close; I haven't checked the time but it seems as if I've been in Rose's garden for longer than I realized. I hear friends saying goodbye to one another. I climb the stairs, am greeted with hello, goodbye, and kisses on both cheeks. I thank Rose, walk back down the steps, out the gate, to my car. *Tomorrow*, I think, *I will be able to look closer.* Tomorrow is another day. From Draymond Green to Scarlett O'Hara. It's been quite a night.

When I talk to Coco the next day, she says, "So how did you like the party?"

"I went slightly crazy," I respond.

"Oh? What happened?"

I recount the Draymond Green facsimile. That I wanted to mow Rose down.

"Sounds like you were triggered."

"Yep," I say.

"And what was the feeling?"

"Frustration. Anger."

"And," she asks, "what was the conclusion?"

"That I was, I am, irrelevant, might as well not exist."

We have just gone through a lightning-fast version of the first three of the six-step process—the trigger, the understanding that "it's about me," and the feeling. Coco asks me to recount an early memory of feeling irrelevant. And I suddenly remember my mother, when I was thirty and told her I was in therapy, asking me if I ever was going to stop gazing at my navel.

I say: "I don't like going back to my childhood. It feels so over. So done. Like going through a garbage can. We've been through the entire basket of my conclusions—I am not enough, I am unlovable, I am doomed. I've already forgiven my mother. It's enough already."

Coco says, "If that were true—if it really were enough already—you wouldn't have wanted to kill Rose."

I recognize that this is true but I don't like it. A minute passes, two minutes.

"You know, Geneen, the level of neglect you experienced was shocking. Your mother treated you as if you were invisible. As if your existence didn't register."

"Oh God," I say. "Here we go."

"Not really," she says. "I'm not sure we've ever gone there."

I take a deep breath, remind myself that belly breathing can activate the parasympathetic nervous system. I need all the parasympathetic help I can get, since hypervigilance seems to be my default mode.

"Let's name the neglect, shine the light on it like sunlight on mold. Tell me another early memory."

I sigh. Do I want to name and see through this pattern or not? Am I willing to viscerally feel the neglect and the feelings underneath it that I seem to have avoided for a lifetime? I see this same reluctance in my students when I suggest they go deeper than telling me "it's just the way it is." They twist their hair around their fingers, wriggle in their seats, and glare at me as if I'd asked them to jump into a leech-filled lake.

"All right," I say. And then I start flipping back in time like I'm rewinding an old videotape.

I'm thinking of my high school journal, which my mother went through page by page, writing arguments in the margins, contradicting what I felt, saw, knew. When I wrote that she was breaking one of the Ten Commandments—thou shalt not commit adultery—she told me I was wrong. Told me she was a good mother.

After I describe this memory to Coco, she asks, "What did you feel when she did that?"

"Erased. Hopeless. It was as if I were living on a planet in another solar system and what I felt or thought or did—that I existed at all—was either a bother or irrelevant to her."

"The fact that she could steal from you, lie to you, and then get furious with you when you confronted her is crazy-making. That she told you that you didn't see what you saw, didn't know what you knew, is so cruel it's breathtaking. But what you decided about yourself is still, *still,* only about you, not about her neglect."

And so it goes: distracting myself from the pain of childhood by creating a different kind of pain.

A chaotic relationship with food was the perfect foil for feeling irrelevant. I binged wildly, dieted mercilessly, and looked and felt mad to all the world but in an acceptable food-centric way. If only I could exert willpower. If only I could eat the right things. If only I could lose weight and keep it off, the madness would (purportedly) disappear; I'd be sane. And I did, I did all of that. I lost weight, I kept it off. I followed the rules. But—maybe it's the moon affecting my mind—I see that wild and seemingly out-of-control patterns with food were expressions of an unspoken, fundamental chaos and so addressing those patterns and their seductive solutions did not fully address their root cause. And although I've been writing about this for decades, and have understood some of this, I haven't understood the roots beneath the roots, the pain beneath the pain. I have never named the fear of madness at the core of me.

"I gotta say," I tell Coco, "I am getting angry at my mother all over again. And I'm starting to feel awfully sorry for myself."

"I understand," she says. "But that is because you are identifying yourself as that child—and you aren't her. You are the awareness that sees her. We are recalling the memory so you can name and dispel the conclusions you've been seeing your life through. *I'm irrelevant. My existence doesn't matter.*

"It is not what happened, sweetheart," Coco says for the thousandth time. "It's what you decided about yourself about what happened. Growing up with your mother was a shitshow, a bad movie. And you are still taking yourself to be the character in that movie.

"But here's the thing: You aren't that character, because you couldn't be telling me about her if you were her. You can get up and walk out of the theater now."

I stand up, try to shake off the agitation and discomfort of hearing again that "it's about me." That it's the conclusion I made about myself from my mother writing in my journal, not the fact that she wrote in my journal. It's not what happened. It's what I believed about myself because of what happened. . . .

Coco adds, "Which is not to say that there is no there there. Those things actually happened, and your body took the hit. Your body registered the assault and armored itself against the chaos and disorganization. And we can turn to it now with kindness and with awareness that you are not it.

"You have a body, you are not your body. You have your conclusions, you are not your conclusions."

Our hour is up, thank God. My brain is sticking together like wet spaghetti. But as soon as I think of spaghetti, I think about meatballs. And as soon as I think about meatballs, I think about garlic bread. Then, suddenly, I am at Mosca's, a restaurant in New Orleans, eating garlic bread and lemon icebox pie for dessert.

Food to the rescue. Food as distraction. Food as comfort.

"I'm giddy," I tell Coco. "I know there is freedom in what you are saying but right now I just want garlic bread."

"Turning to food was a brilliant adaptive behavior," she says. "It kept you from feeling the chaos you had no way of truly being with."

"Yep," I say, "I turned the despair about my parents into the despair about being fat."

"Smart girl," Coco says. "Now you can name and feel the chaos that has been there since you were two or three, chaos that surfaced at Rose's party, and realize you are not it. It's time to put it down."

"Yep," I say again, and step outside into an afternoon light that is so extravagant I want to kneel down to the sky and the puffy clouds that look like mashed potatoes. They are good enough to eat.

CHAPTER EIGHTEEN

Eating My Words

I woke up in the middle of the night recently with a jolt and an *oh no* when I remembered two stories, both of which were about chocolate chip cookies and the guideline I'd been teaching for forty years about eating what you want.

First: When I was a senior in college, my friend Amy and I did what all my women friends and I did together: We dieted, talked about dieting, and binged. Since we lived in New Orleans, where bread wasn't considered bread unless it was fried, we ate fried everything, along with an astonishing variety of sugary foods that were themselves often fried (beignets in the French Quarter, pastries from a bakery on Royal Street, and cookies from a dive we found in Mandeville, on the other side of Lake Pontchartrain). But one day, we decided that we'd had enough with fried treats and it was time to make a new and revised version of Toll House cookies, to which we would add twice the amount of chocolate chips and a heap of coconut flakes.

Since Amy and I wanted to stick to our diets (on the fried-everything diet, you don't eat more than 1,500 calories a day, even if it means eating only half a fried cookie, or five instead of ten beignets), we decided to eat one cookie apiece using our new and ingenious method: We'd divide the entire batch in half, thereby making only two cookies. Amy would eat one half of the batch—one cookie—and I'd eat the other one.

When we sat at her table with the lime-green tablecloth and each ate our allotted cookie, I said, "We sure fooled them." (I didn't know who *them* was, but I did know that she-who-hands-out-gold-stars-for-eating-only-one-cookie-at-a-time was likely befuddled by our scheme.)

Second: When I first stopped dieting, I told myself I could eat what I wanted, and when I asked myself what that was, the only answer was: balls of chocolate chip cookie dough. Since I was determined to follow through on not depriving myself, I spent two weeks eating mostly raw chocolate chip cookie dough balls followed by a gradual introduction of real food: rice, grilled fish, eggs.

Before my foray into unobstructed consumption of raw dough, I felt as if I were stealing when I ate sugary foods. After I stopped dieting, it was as if I'd been unleashed in a candy store at midnight—and everything was free for the taking. It was gleeful. I also walked around spaced out, queasy, flying on sugar, but I didn't care.

Eat What You Want became my motto.

I thought that once I saw, felt, knew that what I wanted would not destroy me, once I gave myself the outrageous kinds and amounts of food I thought I wanted, I'd see that I really did not want them. I'd see that I was rebelling from depriving myself and would eventually want food that wasn't dessert. And it's true, I did, but I was still, as I have written, living at risk of spiraling into a sticky melting heap of negative beliefs about almost everything but particularly who I believed I was supposed to be but wasn't. I was so sure that it was possible to free myself from the hell realm of food-based shame and deprivation by eating what I thought I wanted, which I had never let myself have without guilt, that I didn't bother to question where the wanting came from. I didn't bother to separate the need to stop judging (and its corollary fear that I was a wild animal who, without the imposition of a diet, would devour everything in sight) from food itself. I didn't bother to separate what the eleven-year-old wanted from what *this* body wanted and could thrive on. In those days, there was no thought to whether food energized or drained me, whether it made me feel vibrant or depressed. The fierce determination to break free from deprivation and shame was all the fuel I needed.

Spending two weeks eating raw dough balls is the behavior of someone who believes that she's not allowed to have the kind of sweetness or goodness she wants. Why isn't she allowed to have them? Because she believes her stories about herself, her conclusions about being damaged or wrong or irrelevant or not enough. Until and unless the hunger of she-who-wants-a giant-cookie-or-only-raw-cookie-dough is named and questioned, the wound from which the behaviors/addiction evolved will remain, along with the conclusions and the shame.

Stories from my students:

My mother put me on diet pills at age twelve.

My aunt wrapped my thighs in cellophane twice a week and made me do fifty jumping jacks a day to lose weight.

My stepmother sent me to fat camp when I was fourteen, where they made us exercise in the full heat of the day until exhaustion.

And for years I said I am so sorry about what happened—and as you already have experienced, drugs and jumping jacks and beating the body into shape do not cure the self-rejection that lies beneath those behaviors. Starving the body will not starve the shame of believing, albeit subconsciously, that we don't belong here. To change what you do, you have to question the beliefs and conclusions—I can't be trusted, I'm worthless, I'm needy—from which you do it. And there you stay unless you are willing to take a breath, stop entrancing yourself into how awful it is, was, and will continue to be, and do the work of shining the light on the level of cause: your conditioned beliefs.

When I told myself I could eat what my body wanted, long after the first few weeks of raw dough, visions of blue-and-white Entenmann's boxes filled with coffee cake floated by. Clouds of mashed potatoes, mounds of cupcakes. None of this was particularly conscious. I was not thinking, *Oh, I want coffee cake. Oh, I want mashed potatoes.* I wanted the feeling of being a person who could eat them. A person whose body was whole, intact, respected. Who was allowed to sit at a table without being criticized. Coffee cake became a stand-in for wanting what I couldn't have, and the desire for it felt intuitive, like truly listening to something I had never listened to before.

Feelings of despair and shame had blocked my "intuition" since I started dieting when I was eleven and ate only "dietetic food"—ice milk, plain yogurt, dry cereal without milk—until I ricocheted to bingeing and ate everything that didn't eat me first. It was never a question about which foods would nourish my body, which foods would help my bones grow strong; deciding what foods sustained and enlivened me was not the work of an eleven-year-old, and my mother was focused on my weight, not strong bones.

After a few months eating all the sugary foods I wanted without guilt, I gained weight and then lost it, started small groups in my living room, and stated with confidence that everyone knows intuitively what, when, and how much to eat if they stop shaming and depriving themselves. The key, I said, was to break the diet-binge cycle. It was, I said with certainty, the answer to Everything.

I became evangelical about letting every woman know there was a way out of the shame and punishment of compulsive eating. I preached on *Good Morning America*, *The Today Show*, *20/20*, the nightly news.

Eat dessert first!

Carry a chunk of chocolate everywhere!

Stop eating cottage cheese with friends and a gallon of ice cream in secret!

Above all, trust yourself and your hungers and you will be as healed as someone who has never had an issue with food.

Fast-forward forty years, eleven books, tens of thousands of workshop participants, a decade of working with retreat students, and using myself as an example of someone who was as insane as anyone I've ever met about food, and here is what I now know:

If words were birds and could fly back into my mouth, I'd swallow the ones I wrote about intuitive eating. I would say this instead: Unless an adult is present—someone with discernment, wisdom, and body awareness—any intuition about what, when, and how to eat is based in the past and what we believe we were allowed or not allowed to be, have, and eat.

Once food became my comfort, my drug of choice, a pattern of vulnerability to it and body size was laid down. I still trend to unusual habits and preferences; when my loose jeans become tight, I am alarmed until I remind myself that I am not my body size. Being sensitive to food-related issues does not mean I compulsively eat (except when I do) or that I suffer about food and weight (except when I do).

But so what.

The notion of being healed forever is a myth. As far as I can tell, I keep spiraling around the same challenges (now I call them conclusions), and with each turn of the spiral, I take them less personally. *Oh, there she goes again with food.* I once heard Sylvia Boorstein, a Buddhist teacher, say "I have brown eyes. And I worry," to which I thought, *And I would have given my life for a Hostess Snoball when I was eleven and am still a VVSP (very very sensitive person) around food.*

My relationship with food seems to have stopped developing at the age at which I was judged and shamed for my body. Which means I am twelve getting weighed in Dr. Modlin's office and being shamed about being fat until I realize I am no longer twelve and I begin going back for the pieces of myself that were forgotten.

If an adult isn't at home when the question about what she wants to eat is asked, the answers will be child answers. *I want cookies. I want potato chips. I want a Good Humor Creamsicle.* And saying, "Go ahead, sweetheart, eat what you want," is like telling a twelve-year-old to make herself sick. Note: Taking a drug, any weight-related drug, does not dissolve what the twelve-year-old wants; it either muffles it or changes how much of it she wants. When the drug is stopped, the identity of the child—her pain, her loneliness, her need to be seen—will once again be prominent and so will the desire to eat to repress that wound. Drugs can't erase wounded conclusions. Only turning toward them and understanding that they aren't now, nor were they ever, true will disappear the beliefs/wounds/identities that were installed long before most of us could talk.

Breaking free from compulsive eating does, yes, mean breaking free from the shame and self-loathing associated with it. But eventually I needed to do the work of separating the shame and the sugar. I had to recognize the conclusions that I still believed when I was not allowed to eat what I thought I wanted. It wasn't the weight but what I told myself about the weight that was so painful.

My friend didn't call me back. I knew this would happen. I'm worthless.

I can't stay on any kind of eating plan. I can't even eat intuitively because I am so damaged.

I'm getting old. My neck is sagging. My butt has fallen. I'm ugly.

Again and forever.

When you look at the world through shattered lenses, the world looks shattered.

To eat intuitively in a way that truly nourishes our bodies means listening to a voice unobstructed by child-derived shame or guilt.

It means listening to this body, now.

It means understanding and then acting on what gives you energy and what takes it away. But unless you understand that the voice that speaks loudest is the voice that was silenced decades ago and is yearning for freedom—the freedom of an eleven- or twelve-or fifteen-year-old to choose what she wants to eat because it seems cool or everyone else is eating it or because she wants to get back at her mother for telling her not to eat—you will be listening to the intuition of a toddler, an adolescent, a teenager. Or an adult crazed and hypnotized by the newest weight loss drug.

True intuitive eating means being able to tell the difference between what your body (which is only now and now) wants and what your mind (which is anchored in the past or fantasizing about the future) wants. To eat like an adult, there needs to be a fully functioning adult present—someone who understands the difference between rebellion and acceptance as well as the difference between wanting something because you believe you can't or couldn't have it and wanting it because your body wants it.

Most of us are three- or eight- or ten-year-olds running around in adult bodies, but once you know that you are being swayed by the eleven-year-old with crooked bangs and a longing for her sixth-grade heartthrob Daniel Ashworth to kiss her, you won't be tossed around by the sudden desire for a dozen doughnuts at midnight and call it intuitive eating.

To notice that you are being manipulated by a three-year-old requires a noticer who is not being manipulated. That noticing, that witnessing, is the beginning of knowing who and what you are that is not conditioned by your past, because it is impossible to be both the noticer and that which is noticed. Knowing you are the noticer is the beginning of finding the freedom that is forever sweet—a freedom that does not rely on raw cookie dough.

Everyone eats. Everyone has preferences. Some of us have strong preferences. Shticks, as they say in Yiddish. My aunt Dahlia doesn't like honey. Why? Because her mother forced her to eat it when she was sick. I don't think she's tasted honey in ninety years because the minute the word *honey* is said, she remembers being in bed with the flu when her mother force-fed her honey. Dahlia isn't responding to the honey, she isn't bothered by the taste of honey, she is bothered by her mind's reaction to honey; she is bothered by her thoughts about honey.

The relationship with food is rife with shticks and it's good to know what yours are so that you have a choice about whether to act them out.

What's a shtick?

Eating the best bites first.

Or last.

Moving the peas away from the mashed potatoes so they don't get white fluffy stuff on them.

Not eating fruit with anything but itself because you read a food-combining book when you were fifteen that said you should "eat it alone or leave it alone."

Some people feel self-righteous about their food quirks; they call them healthy. But healthy becomes obsessive when it leads to rigidity and fear, i.e., it's 5:05 p.m. and I start intermittent fasting at five, so I cannot eat one more bite of the falafel I ordered. Healthy becomes obsessive when healthy is a stand-in for the fear of losing control, which itself expresses the fear that you need to arrange your environment so that it is just the way you need it to be, otherwise you will fall apart. Which points to the fear that at your core, you are a chaotic mess.

Another way of saying this is that since there is chaos inside me, I need my environment to be tightly structured, organized, close to perfection, so that the chaos that is me doesn't leak out. So that it never has a chance to rise from the core to the surface. So that no one ever knows what it's really like to walk around inside this body. Who I really am.

I used to believe that the sixth of my seven eating guidelines—eat with the intention of being in full view of other people—was the antidote to the fear that "if they really saw me, they wouldn't love me, therefore I must hide, I must sneak." And to some extent, on the most superficial level, it is. If you hide when you eat pints of ice cream but dine in public on grilled fish and salad without dressing, eating ice cream in front of what feels like the whole universe (but is actually two friends or your partner) will give you a sense of freedom. For a few minutes. But since the way you eat is the way you live and is an expression of deeply held beliefs and fears, eating in full view will not heal the basic conviction that who you are must be locked away, hidden, constrained.

. . .

Even with quirks, shticks, and preferences, there are still and always four stages every one of us passes through in our eating careers. The more quirks, the more pronounced the behaviors in each stage:

STAGE ONE: THE ORIGIN OF INTUITIVE EATING

This stage spans infancy to toddlerhood and is the only true intuitive eating we ever do until we are adults and begin to be aware of the many ways we are still acting like cranky, rebellious children.

Before we are bribed or cajoled, punished for not finishing our broccoli, made to sit at the table until we have finished that last bite of chicken, before sugar ruins our taste buds so that half of us (the other half prefer salty foods) would rather eat sweet things than anything else, our bodies know what they want. They gravitate toward particular foods. My goddaughter, Minnie, wants only broccoli. Her sister, Rona, wants only hamburgers. One of my retreat students remembers wanting and eating only sweet potatoes for three weeks when she was five.

It's all downhill after that, but only for the next thirty or eighty years.

STAGE TWO: COMPLIANCE

This is when eating stops being a response to listening or receiving pleasure or being authentic. When it stops being about satisfaction and begins being about obeying rules.

In this stage, you are told what, when, and how much to eat. You aren't allowed up from the table until you've finished what's on your plate. Your eating is supervised, regulated, measured, not only for nutritional purposes but also because of cultural beliefs, added to what your parents learned from their parents, who learned it from their parents. My mother, as a teeny-tiny example, was told by her mother she was fat. Her mother shamed her. Her mother clucked at the size of her thighs. And then my mother told me I was fat, shamed me, and clucked at the size of my thighs.

Calories in, calories out. Fat is bad. Oat bran is good. Margarine is good for your heart. Margarine is terrible for your heart. Chocolate is healthy. Chocolate has cadmium and lead and is toxic.

This is the stage during which we leave ourselves. We become inauthentic, separate from what we know or want or feel, and because we need love from caretakers, we adapt behaviors that will help us survive. And for the rest of our lives, unless we stop and question our now-automatic habits and the onslaught of information about everything from intermittent fasting to coffee to what causes cancer, we eat like toddlers being hypnotized into dividing foods into good and bad.

And because it is a law of the universe that every diet leads to an equal and opposite binge, the next stage, rebellion, is a reaction to the compliance stage.

STAGE THREE: REBELLION

Two slabs of bread, peanut butter, a banana, a chocolate chip cookie. I'm looking at the plate of a diabetic seventy-five-year-old woman named Rebecca at my retreat during a breakfast eating meditation.

"How old is the girl who decided what to put on your plate?" I ask.

"Seven," she answers. "She was never allowed to eat bread. And even though the doctor says it would be best for my diabetes not to eat this much bread, I don't care. Or rather, she doesn't care. That girl, the seven-year-old, is going to eat what she wants despite what her mother told her or what her doctor tells her. The bread is a way of saying fuck you to my mother, and even though she has been dead for six years, with each slice of bread I say, 'So there, Mom. Watch this, Mom.' "

Until I ask Rebecca how old "the chooser" is, she is convinced she is eating intuitively because she is eating what she believes she wants. By using the excuse of intuitive eating to express the anger of a seven-year-old, she is cut off from what her body needs or wants *now.*

I don't have opinions about what people should or shouldn't eat. I don't have opinions about whether Rebecca should feel the hurt or anger of the seven-year-old and discern what or who is choosing her food.

What I know is that she is suffering in her relationship with food, which is why she came to the retreat. And that she will likely continue to suffer until she can separate food, hunger, and nourishment from ancient wounds. But here comes my opinion: When you pay attention to what is making you miserable, when you name it, feel it, and question it, the misery changes, lightens, and begins to dispel.

STAGE FOUR: FREER AND FREER

Each plate of food is a painting we create a few times a day, an outpicturing of how we feel about ourselves and whether we are in touch with the body we are feeding or entangled in past stories.

Each plate, like each dawn, is a chance to notice if we are here and awake or glazed with stories from the past or fears of the future.

Each plate is a doorway to the inner realms, a doorway to telling the truth no matter what it is: I'm stuck. I'm bingeing. I'm furious. I'm sad.

When I stopped dieting in 1978, I knew immediately, in that first week, that the way I ate was the way I lived. That my relationship with food was an expression of feelings and beliefs I had not been aware of and therefore never expressed. That how I felt about food and eating was the doorway to an entire world I'd long buried. It was the sheer ecstasy that clued me in because I knew it couldn't have just been about allowing myself to eat raw chocolate chip cookie dough. I had touched into the world of deprivation, punishment, shame, trust, and joy, but it took years—and attending multiple meditation retreats—before I understood that when you follow one thing all the way to the end you discover the secrets of the universe. I decided to follow the relationship with food all the way to the end because it had consumed my life until then and I knew that in the reckoning of how I distorted hunger, fullness, joy, nourishment, I could be returned to a basic sanity.

It worked.

It is still working.

I am, you are, we are works in progress.

. . .

The very second you notice—become aware—that you are feeding a seven-year-old, you are a dispassionate observer noticing that you are feeding a seven-year-old. In that untroubled space there are no opinions, no judgments, no preferences. The situation is what it is, that's all. This fork. This hand. This bite. You notice something truer than saying fuck you to a dead mother. Something truer than hurting yourself with each mouthful, than punishing yourself for not being able to stick to an eating plan: ease, calm, peace. And you recognize it as what has been there through every bite, binge, joy, grief, moment of your life, because it is what *registers* every bite, binge, joy, grief, moment.

When I first began meditating, my mind was wild, fragmented, seductive. It wanted me to listen to every thought. *It's urgent,* it said. *You must answer that email now or else . . .*

After forty years of meditating, my mind is still wild, fragmented, seductive; it is still convinced that catastrophe is imminent unless I do what it thinks I should do—now.

I thought that meditating would quiet those thoughts, and for years I was convinced I was a meditation failure—and then I realized that believing I was a failure was just another thought and had no more meaning than "pick up some cheese the next time you go to the market, please."

Awareness is the direct, nonconceptual experience of that which sees your thoughts, beliefs, conclusions. It is who you are without your thoughts.

The purpose of working with conclusions is that when you name them, question them, feel them, you know they are lies; they fall away, and when they fall away, the luminosity of being—of awareness itself—is left.

When you pay attention to the way food tastes in your mouth, you are paying attention to food, yes, but also to that which pays attention: the clear space in which tasting and chewing occurs.

Slowly, with practice, you become aware that you already know this clear place but haven't been paying attention to it because the drama out there is louder. You notice that this wide-open quiet space, not the passing drama, feels like you, like home, like consciousness itself. It may take noticing this ten thousand times, but with each time—the definition of practice is a daily effort to slow down, withdraw attention from the outer world to the inner life—you return and return again. And once you know where home is, you can never unknow.

PART FOUR

The Wound Is the Medicine

CHAPTER NINETEEN

Having What You Already Have

A few years ago I was walking by a store in San Rafael and in the window I saw coasters of hearts with wings. I've always been crazy about heart anything. When I rented my first apartment in Santa Cruz, my friend Lennie helped me decorate my bathroom wall with dozens of heart-shaped boxes. (It was Valentine's Day and stores were replete with heart boxes. I can't remember now what I did with all the chocolate inside those boxes. I had just started weekly groups called Breaking Free from Compulsive Eating, so one would hope that I didn't compulsively eat all the chocolate from those boxes.)

I bought two heart-shaped coasters in the San Rafael store. I gave one of them to my friend Menno, who reminded me of hearts and wings. He loved it. He put it on his home altar when I was diagnosed with cancer. He told me he prayed for me every day.

But still, every time I use the heart coaster, I think, *I want another one. What if this gets lost, broken, ruined? I wonder what the name of that store was. I wonder if it's still open. I wonder if I can call them, ask them to send me a few more.* (It's a mystery how I would lose a coaster I put in the coaster drawer but anyway.)

More. More. More.

I used to do that with food. I'd put some on my plate, take a bite, and before I even finished chewing it, I'd go back for more. What if Matt gobbles it up before I can get more? What if it's all gone and I want more? Do I take more just in case? I have a name for that mind-set: It's called "storing for the hunger to come."

Yesterday, as I was cleaning the other side of the cabinet with the coaster drawer, I found pink wrapping paper, unfolded it, and discovered two more never-used heart coasters. Either I bought four of them that day in San Rafael or they appeared like a gift from Love itself. If I were Caroline Myss, I'd consider that perhaps they just appeared. But since I'm me and I don't have that kind of wonder, I'm left with amazement. And with many questions about "more" and the old belief that there's not enough to go around.

What exactly did I believe would have happened if the coaster broke or got lost and I didn't have another one?

Or if the food I wanted got eaten before I went back?

What is it that I don't want to feel when I keep wanting more of what I already have? Is it emptiness or, in a radical turn, is it realizing the sheer abundance of what is already here?

Here's what I know now: In wanting another coaster, another piece of cake, another soft sweater, I disregard the one I already have. I don't allow myself to really have it, appreciate it. I revert to being a child who believed she didn't have enough love and decided that she needed to take whatever she could wherever she could get it. And I forget to look, to see, to let myself have the contentment that is always already here.

When I was growing up, shopping and eating were equal parts thrilling and shaming. I looked forward to them the way a lover anticipates a forbidden and clandestine meeting: heart pounding with the soon-to-be dive into a world of adrenaline and sensory delights. After my mother and I would shop at My Darling Daughter, we'd sneak the orange heather sweaters and skirts into the house and hide them under the bed so that my father wouldn't see, wouldn't know how much we'd bought (until he got the credit card bill). We knew we'd "been bad" but we liked it. Sneaking and hiding and lying were fun.

When I snuck into the kitchen and hid frozen Milky Ways in my pajamas, I'd eat them quickly, bent over the garbage pail. I'd sneak and hide and lie about eating candy and ice cream and Ring Dings—and then I'd cry from the shame.

I grew up having learned two main things about joy and pleasure. The first was that they weren't free and that I needed to pay for getting what I wanted with guilt and shame. That I needed to hide my appetites.

But the act of hiding and lying and sneaking also taught me that pleasure was *out there,* by acquiring, by eating, by getting more, then more. That by myself, in myself, *in here,* wasn't enough. I needed the doughnut, the sweater, the thing I was not allowed to have to be whole or happy.

And that was a lie. It still is.

CHAPTER TWENTY

Broken Back, Tender Heart

I was about to pick up the teakettle in the kitchen when my legs buckled under me. The pain was so intense I couldn't stand up. So I didn't. I sat on the kitchen floor and looked at the counter, which now seemed impossibly tall and far away. "Siri," I yelled, "call Matt!" One ring, two rings.

"Hi, honey. Something has happened to my legs. I can't stand up."

"Oh no," he said. "I am still forty-five minutes away. Will you be okay until then?"

"I will," I answered. "I'm not in pain now, because I am not moving, so I can keep sitting on the floor."

I looked again at the counter and realized I hadn't looked at my kitchen from that perspective. Ever. The bird whistle in the kettle was tarnished. The counter gleamed where a shot of sun landed.

I thought about calling my neighbors and remembered they were in Phoenix. I thought about calling my other neighbors and remembered they were in Napa for the weekend. So I sat and wandered through pockets in my thoughts about what might have happened to my legs. Where, the second I moved, the pain was coming from. I knew it was not helpful to gallop into the future to *Oh my God am I paralyzed? Will I ever be able to get up?* And so I simply sat.

My erstwhile beloved teacher Jeanne once told me that I did exceptionally well in catastrophes. "It's day-to-day life where you lapse into stories and suffering," she said. And it's true. When I was in a car accident, broke a few ribs, sprained both ankles, I couldn't walk and ended up in a wheelchair for six weeks. I was in pain, yes, and annoyed at Matt when he would wheel me halfway down the hall, get a phone call, and leave me staring at a blank wall. But after a few days, I realized that I only had to do what was in front of me. Look at the wall. Notice the texture of the paint. Breathe. I didn't have to worry about handing in assignments, I didn't have to acquire or achieve or become anything at all. I could just be.

And when we lost thirty years of savings to Bernie Madoff, I quickly realized I had two choices. I could brutalize myself for not diversifying our investments, or I could save myself from torturing myself over having done what I'd already done—and start paying attention to what I hadn't lost: the ability to breathe, to see the hummingbirds drinking from the fountain, to walk with our dog, to revel in Matt's toothy grin. Within two days, I felt richer than I'd felt before we lost our money, because I would not allow myself to wander from this exact step, this moment, this warmth on my right arm—and that was enough. I didn't know how we would pay our mortgage, but I was happier than I'd been in years. So happy that my mother asked if I was on drugs. "It's not normal," she said, "to be so happy after you've lost everything." "I've never been normal," I replied.

I think of this as I sit on the floor, staring at the teakettle and the slants of sun. Then—I have a lot of time—I remember the face of one of my students (emphatically blond hair, green eyes the color of oak leaves), whose husband is dying of ALS. When I talked to her recently, she said, "We didn't deserve this. It's not fair. I don't want to have to deal with this." And my response, along with telling her that I was so sorry, was to say that it wasn't her husband's illness that was causing her so much suffering.

"You might not deserve this," I said, "but it is happening, nonetheless. It might not be fair," I said, "but here it is. Do you keep thrashing around because you don't want what is happening to be happening, or do you breathe, be with your husband, and take care of both of you the best you can? Your choice . . ."

She didn't like that. She wanted to rail about how awful, how horrible it was. Then I asked her how she felt as I talked. She said she noticed that the fist of her stomach unclenched and that she felt somehow better, but she still didn't like or necessarily agree with what I was saying.

As a survivor of multiple catastrophes (Did I mention breast cancer?), I've concluded that the best thing about them is that they present you with two choices: Accept what happened or torture yourself with woulda-coulda-shouldas. Go down in flames or come back to what hasn't been lost or affected by the situation: to the moment, to being present, to peace. Those are always the choices. Ride on the waves of what is happening or fight it and want it to be different.

When Matt walked in, I was still on the floor. He tried to help me up by taking hold of my arms and pulling. I shrieked in pain. Then he tried lifting me up. I shrieked again. The sounds were primal, as if they were coming from an animal. After a few more tries, we realized that shrieking was going to have to be part of getting up. Shriek by shriek we made it to the bed, where I could lie on my side.

Later he said, "You need to eat something," and brought scrambled eggs to the bed. I couldn't turn over or sit up, so I ate them with my fingers. I felt like Helen Keller in the scrambled egg scene of *The Miracle Worker*. I thought, *This is a good way to lose weight*. I could call it the shriek-and-egg food plan.

It's been three days and I still can't turn or move or walk without my legs buckling in excruciating pain. I can't make it to the bathroom or kitchen or to the end of the bed. Since getting to an MRI means the impossibility of putting on clothes, walking to the front door, getting in the car, I don't yet know what is causing the pain—and although the doctor says we could call an ambulance to take me, I decide to wait it out. My heart pajamas are my new best friends.

When I am not shrieking, I feel calm, happy, joyful—which amazes both Matt and me. I begin to understand how much pressure I unconsciously put on myself to do, achieve, produce. How much value I give to accomplishing, succeeding, getting to the end of the day and assessing whether it was a good day or a bad day based on what I did or didn't do. Now, since I can't move, I can't write; and since I can't write, I can't progress on my book deadline. And since I can't achieve, acquire, or become anything, I feel as if someone had given me permission to just *live*. Heaven.

Is being present, I wonder, *the answer to everything?* And my answer is a resounding yes because, here's the thing: In this very moment, despite not being able to walk or move or turn, nothing is wrong. If I don't descend into memory, if I don't compare what I can't do now with what I could do last week, if I don't torture myself with fears of the future based on comparisons with the past, nothing is wrong. There is just this. Pillow under my head. Sound of birds. Green outside the window. I can't move and I am utterly at peace.

I lie in bed looking out the window. The yard is leafy, it is lush, it is sumptuous. We've lived here for twenty-five years, and I can't remember ever looking out this window for more than three seconds while I was making the bed. *I've missed so much*, I think, *in my hurry to get to work*. As if I were getting somewhere important, after which I could finally relax enough to look out the bedroom window.

The wind lifts the leaves and I watch, mesmerized. Was it always this beautiful? Hummingbirds. Dozens of them every day splaying their luminescent wings, reminding me over and over that flight can happen in any moment, every moment. The softness of the breeze as it sways the flowers feels like being kissed, but not in a usual-kiss way. This one kisses my eyes, my arms, lifts the covers. I am in heaven. And then I turn and then I shriek—the pain—and then an adjustment to my position and I am back in heaven.

Still. Giving up being a victim is like chewing nails. I hate it and I love it for the same reason: It eliminates the possibility of blaming someone, anyone else, but most of all, blaming myself.

One night I get all the way to the end of the bed before the pain like an ice pick hacks into my back and I crash to the ground. The glass bowl, the square one with the curved lip in which Matt stores his homemade apple-pear sauce but that is now filled with the night's pee, slips out of my hands. I am still shrieking as I lie splayed on the floor, the pee soaking my hands, my legs, my slippers, the off-white carpet, and my Valentine's pajamas with tiny red hearts. I smell like the back alley at the No-Name Bar.

"Honey?" I say quietly. I hear his soft snores and remember he whom I call *honey* has slept through two earthquakes, one fire, and a standing closet crashing on me in a New Hampshire inn when I reached for a blanket at three a.m.

"Honey," I say, louder this time.

"Hi," he says in a voice blurred with dreams, "where are you?"

"On the floor," I answer. "I didn't want to wake you up and I thought I could make it to the bathroom with the bowl."

I hear the covers being pulled back and then he flips on the light, pads around the bed. Gazes at me, the carpet, the upside-down bowl. "Oh, sweetheart, I'm so sorry," he says. "This is quite a predicament."

The pain has passed and there is a gap between what happened and what to do about what happened. There is no thought that this shouldn't have happened, because it already did. No thought about what this means, because there is no context, nothing to compare it with.

"So," Matt says, "what do you say we get you out of these pajamas?" He puts his arms under my arms and lifts me up, wriggles my legs out of the pajama pants. We wobble inch by inch to the bathroom a few feet away, and I begin to laugh.

"What?" he asks. "What could possibly be so funny now?"

"Remember that question you once asked me about hot water and sex?" I ask.

"I do," he says as we stagger toward the bathroom. "The question was: If you had to give up one of these things for the rest of your life, would you give up hot water or sex? Everyone said they would give up sex."

"Right," I answer, as I shriek-breathe-step. "And the next part was: If you had to give up hot water or laughter, what would you give up?"

"Yep," he says, and grips my back tighter as we reach the threshold of the shower. "No one wanted to give up laughter."

"I chose to keep laughter, too," I say. "But I've changed my mind."

He opens the shower door, turns on the faucet with one hand, and holds me with the other arm, steps in with me. As the hot water streams on my neck, on my legs, my back relaxes and I tell Matt that I am positive that the people who chose laughter over hot water had not just dumped a bowl of pee on themselves.

Today we are determined to make it to the MRI. Getting dressed takes half an hour. Matt has to roll up the socks, slip my foot into each one, and then, leg by leg, arm by arm, help me into clothes.

The hardest part is slipping the compression top, which I wear to alleviate the pain from the lumpectomy, over my head. It is so tight that it bunches up around my neck and we spend many minutes laughing and grunting trying to get it down.

I am newly in awe of anyone who can walk without thinking or shrieking. It feels like walking is what people on planet Earth do and I don't live there anymore.

My first time outside. We are sitting in Matt's car in front of the MRI building. A friend texts me and says, "I am visualizing your spine whole and strong and healed." Hmm, it never occurred to me to visualize my spine healed. I remember that a meditation teacher once told me that I had a pattern he called pre-defeat.

"You give up before you get there," he said. That was fifteen years ago and a lot has changed, but what hasn't changed is that the unavoidable but never true conclusion beneath every other conclusion is: I am doomed. Irrevocably damaged. If I believe I am doomed, there is no point in visualizing a healed spine because, as a doomed person, healing is not for me.

I used to feel this way about breaking free from compulsive eating: doomed, impossible, as if I would always struggle with food. I have mostly cured myself of that. And even before this injury, thoughts of eating when I wasn't hungry all but disappeared. But there is nothing like excruciating pain to take away any remnant desire for ice cream. (I will add, however, and of this I am not proud: Because my appetite has been so radically diminished, my belly is flatter and if I could look in the mirror I know I would see space between my thighs. I know I have lost weight and there is a small, very small but very noticeable, glee about that. I notice the glee, and then I think: *Well, darling, some things might never change*. And then I think: *Oh well.*)

. . .

Coco says you must forgive yourself for believing you were ever doomed—because it is just a conclusion you made up, a belief that you wrapped yourself around. It was unavoidable given your environment but it was never true.

"Can you see that?" Coco asked me. "Feel who you are beneath the belief you are doomed?"

"Maybe," I said. A little. It felt like asking me to separate from my face.

I think of my mother. I think of the ongoing (but ever lighter) story I tell myself about her and me. How when she looked at me, I thought she was disgusted at and by me. Disgusted that I was there, taking up space. It was the very definition of being doomed. Doomed that I was alive. Doomed that I had a mother who didn't want me to be there. The hardest part in this conclusion work is disengaging from my interpretations (i.e., my conclusions) that became the nub of my personality, particularly in relationship to my mother.

I'm not sure what changed—my brother insists it's the drugs, the antidepressant our mother now takes, which seems to have transformed her from seeing what's wrong in any situation to seeing what's right—but now she tells me in every conversation how much she loves me, how in awe she is of my writing. Yesterday, when she called (I didn't mention that I couldn't walk), she said, "I haven't told you recently that you are the diamond in my life, my firstborn, my greatest love. I am so proud of you." When she waxes rhapsodic like this, I remind myself to take it in, as if I were dry toast and she warm honey. I remind myself that my conclusions were only interpretations, my creations, not the truth. And each time I do this, the hard nub of my heart softens and the honey pours in. The conclusion hasn't disappeared, but it is becoming more and more transparent. I feel my mother's love. And I believe her.

Four broken vertebrae and a hairline fracture in my pelvis. Old microfractures turned to major fractures and that was that. The doctor says there is something called kyphoplasty, in which a radiologist injects bone cement into the fractured area and props it up. I'd need to go under general anesthesia to do it. I already can't remember where I put my phone or the word for the green ingredient in pesto. "No," I tell him, "I don't want to do that."

"Then you'll need to wait this out," the doctor says. It will take anywhere from three to six months for these fractures to heal. I can do that. More time to look out the window, more time to watch *Royal Pains* and *Astrid* on the computer while lying in bed. More time to be present. I have a retreat to teach in a month, two classes to teach in two weeks, but for now I keep reminding myself to come back to this sound, this breath, the softness of the pillowcase where nothing is wrong.

When I manage to turn over in bed, I stare at the statue of Kuan Yin, the goddess of compassion and kindness, on our bureau. Sometimes I imagine her getting up and dancing, putting one of her many hands on the floor and, in a Michael Jackson move, spinning and rocking out to Bobby McFerrin's "Don't Worry Be Happy."

Wanting this to change, wishing it didn't happen, galloping

into the future, would be living hell. (I've quoted Buddhist teacher Stephen Levine for years: "Hell is not fire and brimstone, not a place where you are punished for lying or cheating or stealing. Hell is wanting to be something and somewhere different from where you are.") I deeply resonate with this desire to think or wish or push myself to be somewhere and someone different than I am. To be someone who is less triggered by certain situations, less contracted in her heart, less attracted to sugar.

But as I lie here, I know without a doubt that resistance to this situation really is the definition of suffering because there is not a thing, not one, I can do about the pain (except take drugs, which I am doing, without significant relief) and if I fight it or fear it, my mind becomes like a steel clamp and my body gets even tighter. I ask myself, over and over, *How is this for me, not against me? If I had orchestrated this, what would I have wanted to see or know that I don't see or know now?*

My student whose husband is dying of ALS told me that when she allowed herself to stop ranting about how unfair it was, she realized there was still so much of her husband left and that she was missing him by wanting another version of him back. She was missing her current life by wanting the life she used to have. "When I touch his hair or watch him laugh or help him walk, I am perfectly happy."

Coco often says, "Imagine you woke up and the part of your brain that records memories was gone. You can't remember your name or your mother's face or, for that matter, anything at all. But you can see, feel, hear, walk, touch, taste. Would anything be wrong?"

Nope. Nothing. Because nothing is ever wrong in this exact moment.

It's a lesson I have to keep learning over and over. You probably do, too.

I spend days staring out the window and looking at the ceiling. Years ago, I asked my friend Shawn to paint the sky on our ceiling so that we could look up and see clouds and blue always. Now when I am not watching the wind, I sky-gaze.

I remind myself of a story Byron Katie told in one of her books, when she was visiting a woman with cancer who had one leg that was swollen to twice the size of the other. But my leg, my leg the woman said, after which Katie said, "The only thing that is wrong is that you believe your legs should be the same size."

Every time I remember that story, I know that nothing is wrong. My back is in pain and nothing is wrong, it is just the way it is. For now, I am aware that when you can't get around easily, you have to be still. And that when you have to be still, you have a chance to notice stillness. This is a portal to quiet. To space. This is my chance to put down the *have to*s and *want to*s. *Take it before it passes,* I whisper to myself so I don't put myself under the spell of how awful, how horrible, what a catastrophe this is.

Friends call. I say, "*Thank you for calling, I love you, and let me call you* when I want to talk." I don't want to explain that this current situation is a portal to presence itself. I experience the freshness of morning. The sun on my face.

This latest mishap allows me to notice the mind-trance in which I often live and how I am still obeying instructions—of course this was going to happen, things always fall apart, you messed up big-time, not sure how or when but this whole thing has got to be your fault, catastrophes and chaos are what everything always comes down to—given to me sixty years ago by people I wouldn't ask for street directions from today.

I wait. I recover, and as I do, here is what I notice: When there is great challenge to either the mind or the body, and I don't immediately swirl down into "this shouldn't have happened," my attention is forced to be present. Every moment is exactly what it is, nothing added. It's like waking up without a past, without a memory of how hard it was, how awful, who did what and what I should or shouldn't do. There is nothing but this and this and this. It's such a blessed relief to drop the heaviness of beliefs and stories, of grudges and melancholy.

The hardest part of the day is sitting up after sleeping. I still can't do it without shrieking. Matt puts his hand behind my back to act as a human compressor belt and, slowly, we inch up to sitting. And then walking. One hand gripping a cane, the other arm held by Matt.

Once I am upright in the mornings—a process that takes ten, fifteen, twenty minutes because I shake and fall back down many times—I take the cane and walk. My legs feel wooden, like Pinocchio legs. Wobbly and uncertain. I must look like I am drunk as I weave to one side and then the other but I am so happy to have legs that can walk. Matt opens the back door and I take a step down. The smell of the white star jasmine climbing the trellis is transportive, like getting on a rocket ship and landing in a lush green world where beauty grows in every crack and crease, fills every breath, and is all that matters.

I maintain a holy vigilance to not wander in the hell realms of my mind. The air itself is new, fresh, lush. On the hillside there is a fusillade of wild iris, waves of violet and pale yellow. And the poppies! Meteor showers of saffron light. That is all that is happening now. Only that.

We need to cancel a trip to Kauai because sitting for five hours on a plane is as doable as running the Boston Marathon. We paid for the rental condo months ago, didn't get trip insurance, and now cannot get a refund. "Let's give it away," I say to Matt, in an uncharacteristic gesture. "Which one of our friends would like a free trip to Kauai?" We offer it to our friends Lucy and Robert, who act as if they have won the lottery. My tough lychee nut heart, the one that believed it didn't have enough to give away, feels like it's broken open. Is crazy with love. They—ahem, it was Paul quoting Jesus—were right: Giving is as good as receiving. (I know, I know. Paul said that it was MORE blessed to give than to receive but I haven't reached the "more" stage.)

My mind is utterly quiet—a state I've tried and often failed to reach in meditation. But recently, even before this, uh, injury, Coco insisted that who we already are *is* meditation itself. That when we stay out of the bad neighborhoods of our minds, we are peace itself. And now that a catastrophe has (once more) given me permission to be vigilant about not wandering into those neighborhoods, the sweetness of peace keeps washing over me. If I can feel ecstatic with four broken vertebrae, then that kind of happiness is available always. I know the "always" part sounds like a stretch. Like hyperbole. Like a promise to explore in a book.

Well, I'm here to say once again that if I can do this—and it's not a doing, it's a being—so can you. And the first step is to want it enough to imagine it, which takes naming what it is in you (a conclusion) that doesn't believe it's possible. And then, deciding on a practice, an action, you can do every day, fifty times a day, to inscribe that in your brain. It could be as simple as taking three deep breaths every half an hour, since you have to breathe anyway. But it has to be something you actually do—because if you want different results, you need to do different things, and without the urgency of a catastrophe that ejects you out of your routine, you get pulled under the tow of familiar habits and the daze of slogging through to-do lists.

For more than thirty years I've loathed the word *discipline* because it connotes dieting and we all know how I felt and still feel about dieting. And I've been espousing hearts, flowers, and compassion about instituting practices, believing that compassion is what we all need, not more routine, not more discipline. But, once again, I'm eating my words.

I'm done with (only) hearts and flowers and flowy this and that; being inspired is lovely, but it does not lead to transformation. When I first started breaking free from compulsive eating, I kept a list of every bite I put in my mouth and what I was feeling before I ate and how the food affected me. It worked because by writing, I became a witness to what I was doing, and in becoming a witness, I was able to disengage from the hand-to-mouth momentum and catch myself in the moments before I ate to ask myself if I really wanted food at that moment. So, I have been giving writing assignments (some might call it homework—horrors) to my retreat students. "Write down how many times you ate compulsively today and tell me what the benefit was, because if you didn't believe it was helping you, you would stop doing it." And "Tell me the excuses you give for not following through. Write them in a list and then send them to me." I ask each of them to commit themselves to an everyday practice of dropping out of their mind and into their heart. It could be setting a timer on their phone that rings every hour, after which they stop, put their hand on their chest, and breathe three times. It could be spending fifteen minutes a night gazing at the night sky. It could be—and is—anything that stops the incessant flow of thoughts and reminds them to look, see, breathe. "It's time to get going, girls," I say. "If you want different results, you need to do different things."

They don't like this new version of me. They look at me like I've turned into Cruella de Vil. They, most of them, don't do the homework. And my response is: "I love you anyway and always." And "The way you do or don't do the homework is the way you do your life. The excuses you give for not following through show up in every area of your life." I repeat, "If you want different results, do something different." Then I add: "By the way, Cruella wanted to kill ninety-nine dalmatians, but I only want to kill the ways you turn against yourself. So," I say, "get your ass in the chair and send me your homework."

My favorite place to walk is outside, so in the mornings, as soon as I grab the cane, I wobble to the back door and I walk and I walk. Two times around the courtyard, pretending I just arrived here on Earth and am seeing all this green for the first time. I forgot that the tree that wasn't leafing was a dogwood, and for the first week I thought, *Oh, it died during the winter. The branches are so bare.* Then, suddenly, a few green leaves appeared, but just a few. And then more and more, and one day a pale pink flower was there and the next day another one and I thought that I would die from the beauty. That, to paraphrase Mary Oliver, I would be killed with delight over and over with each flower, cloud, birdsong until there would be nothing left but delight, beauty, joy. What a way to die . . . and all it takes is seeing what you see, being where you are, loving what you love. This includes matcha lattes, chocolate, and, yes, even the lilt of my mother's voice when she calls me darling.

It's been three months since that leg-buckling day in the kitchen. I am able to walk a few miles a day on a flat surface, able to make the bed, my breakfast, do the things that people who can walk can do.

Part of what I've been practicing for healing my spine is remembering an activity I adored that required a strong spine, seeing myself doing it, feeling the way I felt when I did it, and adding a physical movement to represent it so that I can inscribe it in my body. (I read this protocol in a RJ Spina book.)

For the first few weeks, I was picturing myself walking on my favorite beach at sunrise and feeling the elation at seeing the colors. Now I can actually do that, so I am moving on to more vigorous activities—like dancing.

Dancing. I had forgotten about dancing. The blue tutu with the rainbow-colored tulle skirt, my toe shoes, my tap shoes. Dancing with my father and brother at the yearly recital that Sandy Murphy, our dance teacher who was also a Rockette, produced. Doing African dance, which I did three times a week when we lived in Santa Cruz. It was wildly exuberant, incredibly joyful. Live drummers, moving up and down the room as the group of us danced across the floor. I see it now, the laughter, the exertion, the sweat pouring down my strong back, and I feel the glee of dancing. I put on "Wouldn't It Be Nice" and suddenly I am twenty years old again and anything is possible. I think of Dick's mother, Dorothy, when we stood in the den as I taught her some African dance moves. She was wearing a red knit dress as she fluttered her arms to the beat of the drums.

I start moving in a creaky way, little movements of my arms, but what I imagine is leaping, what I imagine is waves of joy floating off my resilient body.

CHAPTER TWENTY-ONE

Crossing Over

It is morning, seven a.m., and I am making breakfast: two spoonfuls of matcha, a cup of pumpkin seed milk, a teaspoon of cinnamon and cardamom, turmeric paste with black pepper, a tablespoon of green-everything powder, and hot water. (Before we sleep, Matt and I list the wonders of the day. Along with the thrum of hummingbird wings, our dog Izzy's prance, a sprig of daffodils, I add: "And my morning matcha was sublime. It was better today than ever." I've been saying this every night. For five years.)

The phone rings as I am adding the turmeric. My mother is calling and I decide to put my breakfast aside and pick up, since the last time I talked to her, on the third anniversary of Dick's death and after she told me how much she loved me and how proud she was of me, she said she was unbearably lonesome and no longer wanted to live. She said that every bone in her body ached to see me. When I told my brother, who lives a few minutes from her, he said, "Yeah, yeah. She told me that, too, and then told me she needed a manicure, a haircut, and that she *must must must* have a new pair of pants."

"Do you have a minute?" she asks.

I add the turmeric and the water. Blend the mixture.

"Sweetheart," she says, "I want to talk to you. I have been thinking about the past and I wanted to tell you I am sorry."

"For what, Mom?"

"For being a terrible mother. For only caring about myself and what I looked like. For spending so much time on my clothes and my appearance that I neglected you and your brother. For thinking makeup was more important than you."

I pour the matcha into my striped mug with the raised heart on the front. I marvel at how green green can be. I pull up one of the rattan dining room chairs and sit. I am mute but not in a bad way.

When my mother used to hit me, when she was red-faced and the vein in her forehead was pulsing, I would carefully compose my face into a wall. Hard. Expressionless. Cold. I wanted her to believe she couldn't touch me; it was the only control I had, and because I knew it would make her crazier, it was also a way of hurting her back. "If you don't say something, I am going to send you flying into the middle of next week!" she'd scream. Still, I was mute, frozen, catatonic.

Now on the phone, she says:

"You are the diamond in my life. My firstborn."

"I love you more than life."

"I am so proud of you and all you have accomplished."

"I didn't know how to be a mother."

"I was starving to be loved. Your dad and I were so unhappy."

"Can you ever forgive me?"

"I don't want to die with regrets."

I spent my life waiting for my mother to save me from my mother. Now I am saving myself from turning against myself.

She says, "I love you so. I am so sorry for missing all the years you were growing up. For not being there when you needed me."

"Mom," I say, "I am glad for you that you are looking back on your life. And I don't know what to say. But I do believe you love me as much as you can. Can we have a part two of this conversation, because it's a lot to take in."

She says, "Yes, sweetheart."

I drink the matcha. I toast a tortilla, slather it with ghee.

Have I been blind to the love that she feels for me now because I have been so convinced of the love I didn't feel from her then?

Yup. But in my own crooked defense, it's been seven decades of shielding myself from her relentless criticism.

After I hang up the phone, I decide to take another look at the needlepoint tapestry in our hallway that my mother sewed when she was ten years old and living in a small Bronx apartment. I can imagine her, a ten-year-old, sitting patiently and cross-stitching blue thread through fabric, spelling out the word *God*. Then *Bless*, then *Our*, then *Home*. When I look at that needlepoint, I see the girl who created it, the hope that she would have a loving home. I see innocence. I see a bewildered child whose mother told her she was too fat. I see the child who lives in my mother's now ninety-three-year-old body. The child who never got the love she craved.

My mother says her mother took her shopping in the "chubby" section of Macy's. Criticized her body. Looked at her with accusing eyes. And then my mother passed it on—the body comments, the criticism, the love withheld—to her daughter. To me.

God Bless Our Home is hanging in the hallway of my home now. I see it as soon as I walk in the door and it reminds me that everyone was someone's baby. Everyone starts out innocently, wanting to be welcomed, cherished, gazed at with tenderness. It also reminds me that until we acknowledge, accept, and somehow find room to welcome the one who didn't receive that love, we never grow up. We stay toddlers in big bodies.

I think about my mother's phone call, about hearing all the things I'd always wanted her to say. She is kind now, but it's not her kindness that has changed me; I've learned (most of the time) to be kind to myself, to, as Mary Oliver writes, "love sorrow," and in loving it/my mother, I allow myself to grow, I become an adult.

I walk past the front door, out to the courtyard, and I realize that taking in love now means unshriveling my heart. Means not protecting it from the onslaught of what I perceived as her disgust of me. And as Coco reminded me tens of times: It's not that your mother wasn't neglectful. It's not that she didn't hit you. But and still: All you ever experience now is who you are being to yourself.

I scroll through the texts my mother has written in the past few years. I see love. I read love. I hear that she is loving me as much as it's possible for her unshriveling heart:

Nov 21

Had a fun dream about you last night—can't wait to tell you about it I love you so much

Nov 14

How is the zoom program doing . . . are you happy with it. I miss talking to you about everything . . . you know how much I love the sound of your voice . . . I love you so much. Not talking to you makes me ever more lonely . . . much much love [heart] hugs [three hearts, two exclamation marks]

Feb 11

Love you so much think about you all the time . . .

July 22

Miss you too much love you and ache to see you . . . sometimes could cry because I really haven't seen you in forever . . . love you love you love you, mommy

Feb 6

Hi my Delicious child . . . just wanted to say hello to you and say I love you [two hearts] Mom

March 24

Have I told you lately how much I love you [hearts] and how much I love talking to you . . . Mom

March 29

Your Facebook entry is really inspiring . . . you look so very beautiful. Love you so much [kiss, heart] and hope you will always be happy and healthy . . . I am so glad to be your mom.

April 3

Tried to FaceTime you . . . so sorry I couldn't reach you . . . love you very much and will never stop trying!! [three hearts, smiley face, face with hearts]

Six months after the apology phone call, we move my mother into an assisted living facility fifteen minutes from her apartment. She resisted moving, told me I'd have to carry her out of her apartment feetfirst, that there was no way she was moving "into a facility." It took exactly one week for her to realize that being around other people lifted her depression. Now she is not lonely. Now she doesn't have to worry about shopping for food or making her bed or having as much money as her friend Mitzi has. Now I tell Coco, I know what being enlightened means: My mother doesn't want what she doesn't have and wants only what she does have. Keds that are forty years old. Bracelets from Target. Gray potatoes at lunch.

She has a roommate named Marilyn with "big hair and a loud voice" and although their room is tiny with only one window, my mother is convinced it's the best room in the whole place. This proclamation from a woman who spent ten thousand dollars on a mirrored chest for her never-big-enough apartment.

And there's this: Ginger, the entertainment director, is putting on a Ms. Super Senior America Pageant and has asked my mother to be the star. She will wear a (borrowed) sequined blue top with a gold fringed skirt and talk to the residents about why she is at peace and how they, too, can be at peace.

"At peace?" I ask my mother. "Really? You have become a model citizen for peace?"

"Yes, I suppose I have. Because after all this, after the miserable marriage with your father, after forty happy years with Dick and after believing I never had enough of anything—watches, earrings, shoes, sweaters, couches—all that matters to me now is peace."

When I talk to my brother about this peace business, he once again says, "It's the drugs. She's finally on an antidepressant."

I laugh, say, "I am certain they are contributing, but I know quite a few people who are on drugs and are still sort of miserable." He is not so sure.

But I am. Because she is happy being happy. Because the definition of happiness is not resisting what's in front of you. Is not wanting to be anywhere else. Because when you are here, really here, nothing is wrong. And this is what my mother is now teaching me: Inconceivable change is possible. Is here now.

CHAPTER TWENTY-TWO

Love, Finally

My mother calls on FaceTime as I am making the bed. I am seventy-one, she is ninety-four.

"Hi, Mom," I say. "I'm going to put the phone on the bedside table while I finish making the bed."

"Hospital corners?" she asks, noticing how I am tucking in the sheets. "You're making hospital corners? You never learned that from me."

"I learned it at camp from the military guy, George. He'd throw a quarter on our beds and if it didn't bounce, we'd have to start all over with those stiff white sheets and scratchy gray blankets."

"Forget George," she says. "I'm your mother and I'm telling you that you never have to make another hospital corner again."

"What a gorgeous mirror," she says, pointing to the gold antique mirror above the dresser.

She notices every detail: my latest haircut, a painting of an owl with a gold crown, the antique mirror on the wall.

I fluff the pillows, pick up the phone, and gaze at her face. For the past six months she has worn no makeup at all, after putting on what she called "her face" (concealer, eyeshadow, rouge, eyeliner, mascara, lipstick) every day for eighty years. She looks washed clean of the past; I can see the face beneath her face for the first time.

"You have on makeup," I say. "That's different than what you've been doing."

"Yes," she says, "it's the eyeliner I got in the penny store downstairs. I feel good. Now tell me where you got that mirror."

"At a garage sale. Now tell me about your new friends."

"There are four of us and we call ourselves the CRABs. It's an acronym for our names: Carole, Ruth, Arlene, Bonnie. I am the oldest CRAB of all."

"It's so great you've made some new friends, Mom. What do you do together?"

"We play Rummikub and bingo, and go to the entertainment events together. The other day they had Hawaii Day."

"Okay," I say, "I'll bite. What is Hawaii Day?"

"It's when they decorate the ceiling with hundreds of different-colored balloons and play Hawaiian music. No hula skirts, though, because most people can barely get out of their wheelchairs. They pound their canes to this music instead.

"And the CRABs kibitz," she says. "In fact, yesterday Bonnie told me how spiritual her daughter is, and I said, 'You want to know spiritual? You have no idea what spiritual is until you've met my daughter.' "

I howl with laughter. "Is it spiritual," I ask, "to tell her that your daughter is more spiritual than hers?"

"Who cares about that," she says. "You know, sweetheart, I can't believe I'm going to be ninety-five. I really thought it was going to take longer to get old."

"Yeah," I say, "who knew it would go by so fast?"

"By the way," she says, "I meant to tell you this: When I melted down last summer and forgot everything, I only remembered two things: your birthday and your brother's birthday. The doctor thought that was significant. I did, too. I love you two so much.

"I have to get off the phone now. My CRABs are waiting. Bye, honey," she says, and kisses the phone while making a big smacking sound.

As I pad to the kitchen to drink the remaining matcha latte, I notice that my chest feels like melted gold; the heart-wall seems to have disappeared. I start humming a version of the Lost Boys line from *Peter Pan*—"We have a mother, at last we have a mother. At last we have a mother"—and suddenly understand that what I actually have is not her mothering now but what I thought I would have if I had the mother I thought I wanted: kindness for this body-mind, confidence that I belong here, a path back to myself when I feel lost, peace.

Love without a story.

Love that carries no risk of being harmed.

Love that has no walls, no edges.

Love that meets itself in love.

CHAPTER TWENTY-THREE

The Wound Is the Medicine

I was eleven when I stood in front of the mirror for hours singing the Hayley Mills song "Johnny Jingo." I pursed my lips. I rocked my hips. I pretended I had long blond hair and I belted out the words. A thousand times a day. I wanted to *be* Hayley Mills. But what I wanted most was to be seen, and by being seen, to be loved. At first, I thought that being an actress would make me famous, which would allow me to be both seen and loved. When only the theater teacher clapped at a school performance of me in a play, I realized I was never going to make it as an actress and decided to be a model instead. I changed my name to Geneen Howard and dragged my brother to the Barbizon school in Manhattan, where they weighed me and told me I was too fat and too short. Then I decided that all I really needed was to be thin because if I was thin, my mother would love me—and my obsession with being seen became my obsession with being thin.

Recently a doctor told me that my DNA test revealed that I should have been, had the genes to be, fat. "I don't understand it," she said. "Every gene for physical size and weight points to you being fat. I've only seen this aberration once."

That's me, I thought. *Aberrant all the way.*

To what do I attribute this anomaly?

To what (I know I am going to get in scientific trouble for this) goes beyond genes and this physical vehicle we call the body: to working through so many issues about food and hunger for the past forty-plus years that I am no longer snagged by any of it (except when I am). I attribute it to clarity. To perseverance. To presence itself.

I never believed in the theory of fat cells or set point or that once you diet, your metabolism goes into starvation mode and it's therefore easier to gain weight when you stop dieting. I knew without a doubt that my relationship with food went far beyond physical causes. Even when I wrote my first book, *Feeding the Hungry Heart*, I knew that the causes of what I did with food were invisible.

What I didn't know then was that my behavior was a result of thoughts and beliefs, which themselves were a result of judgments and conclusions I made about myself before I could talk. I didn't realize how deep the self-abandonment was. I didn't realize that untangling it was a process that takes awareness and challenging deep-seated beliefs and that new patterns of thought, action, and behavior arise as a result.

. . .

I became a writer because I loved writing. But when that writing turned into books, my dreams about being an adult version of Hayley Mills, i.e., being seen, resurfaced. And I transferred my dreams of being famous to being on *Oprah*. I still believed that if enough people saw me, I would be healed. I would be loved and the self-rejection would dissolve.

My first bookstore reading for *Women Food and God* was at Copperfield's Books in Petaluma, California. The room was set with fifty chairs; four people showed up, two of whom were friends. "Not a promising beginning," I told Matt on the way home. "I'm awash in *D* feelings—dejected, depressed, discouraged, disappointed, disconsolate, despondent. Have I left anything out?"

A few weeks later my friend Elizabeth Lesser, who was a frequent host of *Oprah's Soul Series* radio show, gave my book to Oprah, who loved it. And after hearing the news, I shrieked with excitement, scared the dog, and the two of us ran around the courtyard ten times, awash in the opposite of the *D* words: energized, ebullient, exultant, enthralled, electrified.

Oprah's producer asked if I could come to Chicago and tape a few episodes of *Soul Series* with "Ms. Winfrey."

Could I sit in a studio with Oprah for a few hours?

Give me a moment. . . .

Yes, I said, and I thought: *Is there a plane leaving in ten minutes?*

I wore Frye boots to the taping. She wore ballet slippers. I was bedazzled. She was welcoming. We sat in the studio for a few hours, after which she asked me how many books my publisher had printed. A few thousand, I answered. They were reluctant to print more. "If you get them on the phone, I'll talk to them," she said. It took three seconds for me to call Susan Moldow, the publisher of Scribner. When she answered, I said, "I have someone who would like to talk to you," and handed the phone to Oprah. "Susan? This is Oprah Winfrey," she said, and then after a few niceties, "It's time to print a few hundred thousand books."

I was standing in the doorway of Oprah's office and started jumping up and down waving my arms like an unruly patient released from the asylum. "Thank you," I said. "I don't know how to thank you." Oprah laughed, said, "You are very welcome." I told myself to calm down before she and her producers decided I was not fit for television.

When a date was set for my appearance on the show, I did what any girl would do before she appears on national television—I bought a new outfit. But when I tried on my new shoes in the dressing room on the morning of the show, the box had two left shoes. Oprah's producers called Neiman Marcus and within ten minutes there was a stack of eight new pairs of shoes. The only pair that fit me, though, had heels so high I couldn't walk. No problem, the producers said, we'll have you carried out to the stage. A few minutes before the show started, two men, one on each side, lifted me by the elbows a few feet off the floor and whooshed me into my seat.

Oprah was funny and engaging, I was agog with excitement and still managed to speak in whole sentences. It was like the moment I met Nelson Mandela in South Africa when he was made president and sputtered, "I am so honored to meet you." He smiled and said, "Thank you. You are very kind. I like your earrings."

The line was out the door for my next book reading. And the ones after that. Hundreds of people were turned away. I was incredibly grateful that more and more women were discovering there was a way out of compulsive eating that didn't include punishment or deprivation. Also, although Matt and I had lost our money to Bernie Madoff the year before *Women Food and God* was published, and although Annie Lamott told me we could move in with her if I left my sweaters somewhere else, Oprah Winfrey's endorsement meant we could now pay our bills. But even Oprah's endorsement didn't take away the background sense of being the wrong person to be living my life. I still woke up a few times a week glazed in a caul of melancholy and comparative judgment: I wrote the wrong book. I live in the wrong house. I said the wrong thing. Sometimes, not often, I'd hit the bottom of the barrel of discontent and convince myself I married the wrong man.

Ellen DeGeneres said: "I didn't go into this business for money. It was about healing my childhood wounds. I thought, if I can make people happy, then they'll like me. And if they like me, I'll feel good about myself, and all I can say about that is: Thank God for the money."

When I met Matt, he told me that he was going to love me like no one had ever loved me. And he did. And he does. But I didn't know that no one person, not even twenty-six million of them who watched the *Oprah* show, could erase childhood wounds.

I started writing *Love, Finally* after meeting Coco and realizing I was still mucking around in being a victim, still blaming my mother, still turning against myself in a thousand ways. In Coco I met a human who was very human—thick ankles, egg stains on her shirts, jiggly thighs—and not human at all. During the six years I've known her, I've watched her deal with Covid and obstreperous people, and she's become increasingly blind, but not once have I detected a note of defensiveness or ego. Not once. And if it is possible for her, it is possible for me. For you.

Now when I am convinced that I am the universal exception, that what I am feeling is not about me, I know it's about me—and after I question the conclusions, a fundamental sense of well-being and ease returns.

And that's how it goes. Days, weeks, months of soaring, of feeling boundless and free and not torturing myself with self-rejection and then crashing to the ground and hating my mother and believing I'm a victim and then brushing myself off, questioning my thoughts, and bringing myself back to this moment where nothing is wrong.

And if you are thinking you need a Coco to change the way you look at things, you have one. It's you. Because I know without a doubt that no body size, no fortune, no fame, no relationship will heal the wound you are seeing through; it was/is your creation and only you can discreate it. (Go ahead and roil and thrash, and after you do that, remember what you want most of all.)

The wound doesn't need to meet the medicine, as I thought when I first met Coco; the wound *is* the medicine.

I can't think of anything, not one thing, more important to do than question what we believe about ourselves, the people around us, and the world we experience. And simultaneously question the connection between who we think we are based on conditioning and who we are when that conditioning falls away. Because when we look "out there," read the news, listen to podcasts, it sure seems like the world is a mess—as if chaos, hopelessness, violence, political corruption, and climate catastrophe are facts of life. But out there is made of people who are acting out their "in here's"—their ongoing hopelessness, self-neglect, refusal to be kind to themselves—and as far as I can tell, one of the most effective ways to change out there is to change in here. If I don't walk around afraid, convinced I have enemies, believing in us versus them, if I don't walk around knee-deep in self-hatred, I won't use food or drugs or guns or alcohol or hatred to vanquish the demons because there won't be demons. Imagine that. No demons in here, no demons out there.

When I practiced "Johnny Jingo" a hundred million times, all I wanted was love, and I believed that if I got it out there, I would feel it in here. I couldn't have known then that it was always mine.

It takes a lifetime to return to where we've always been.

CODA:

IF I HAD A DAUGHTER

On a foggy morning three months after my twenty-seventh birthday, I decided to kill myself. I was sitting on the floor in my light blue flannel cloud pajamas surrounded by empty cartons of Breyers vanilla fudge ice cream and three-cheese pizza boxes—remnants of my nightly twenty-thousand-calorie binges—when the phone rang and I heard my mother's voice on the answering machine.

"Sweetheart?" she said. "I haven't heard from you in a while. Please call me."

I roused myself from the floor, stumbled to the bedroom, picked up the handle of my baby-blue princess phone.

"Hi, Mom," I said, voice blurred with tears.

"What's wrong?" she asked.

Before I thought about what I was saying and to whom, I blurted, "I'm lost. I hate organic chemistry and physics. I thought going back to school and taking premed courses so that I could be a doctor was a good idea, but I was wrong—and I don't know what else to do with my life. So I eat. And then I eat more. I've gained eighty pounds and am fatter than I've ever been. I want to kill myself."

"Darling," she said calmly, "you are beautiful no matter what you weigh."

I wanted to believe her, but she had been telling me I was fat since I was eleven and her voice then had become my voice now: *You're fat. You're ugly. You're disgusting.* Hearing her say I was beautiful no matter what I weighed was astonishing, relieving—and impossible to believe. It was as if she had suddenly shape-shifted into the mother of my dreams.

"You don't believe that, Mom. What about all those years you told me I needed to lose weight?"

"I do believe that. Your face lights up my whole life. And I am sorry I don't tell you that more."

"But, Mom, I can't stop eating."

"You will," she said, "when it's time. And you will find what you want to do. You're only twenty-seven. Quit what's making you miserable and find what you love."

"What if I never find what I love to do?"

"You are wise beyond your years, sweetheart. I trust that wisdom, honey. You can trust it, too. If you relax and stop being so hard on yourself, I'm certain you will discover what you most want to do."

"I'll try, Mom. Let's talk in a day or two."

For most of my life, I'd been terrified of my mother's rage, but when she married Dick when I was nineteen, she soaked in his buttery glow. "I am the luckiest man in the world," he'd crow, looking at her as if we needed sunglasses to shield our retinas from the blinding magnificence of her presence. And although this post-binge conversation was unusual—both because I was unusually desperate and because I didn't usually talk with her about my weight—it was now I who was soaking in the butter-love.

I gazed at the empty cartons on the floor, aware that the desire to kill myself had dissipated. One by one, with each crumpled package I asked myself what I would do if I could throw away my textbooks and do anything in the world. The answer came immediately, as if it had been waiting for me to notice it: *Write.* I would write. I had no idea what I would write, only that I would. Until then, I'd been the straight-A student who does what is expected of her. But when I began crumpling the second carton of Breyers ice cream, I remembered Mrs. Epstein, my fifth-grade teacher. Her chestnut hair, her enthusiasm for trying new things like playing the recorder and buying one share of Pan Am stock. On the day she asked us to write an essay about a girl hero, my new Bic pen flew across the page and I wrote about a fifth grader—me—saving a plane from crashing when the pilot fainted. As each word appeared on the page, thoughts dissolved, feelings from that morning's fight with my mother faded, leaving a sense of wholeness and belonging. I'd never experienced anything like it before. I was not a bookworm. I read Nancy Drew books and the Bobbsey Twins, not books by Charles Dickens or poems by Emily Dickinson. I liked Barbie and Ken dolls, not retreating to my room and disappearing in short stories of my own creation. Writing found me that day in Mrs. Epstein's class but I never, for one moment, imagined I could be a real writer.

After that conversation with my mother, I quit my premed courses and began taking a weekly class called Writing About Our Lives, taught by Ellen Bass. Ten women and I sat in a circle while Ellen—with her halo of frizzy dark hair and easy laugh—encouraged us to write an essay about the breakup of a relationship for the following week.

At home, I sat at my oak kitchen table with the wobbly legs and wrote about growing up in New York—"the lights of the Empire State Building all I knew of stars"—and breaking up with my boyfriend of nine years. I labored over that piece for hours but when I brought it in the next week, Ellen kindly tore it apart. "More detail," she said, "and far fewer adjectives." Undaunted, I took it home and worked on it for more hours. It was all I wanted to do. When I wrote, my usual self disappeared and I felt as if I was doing what was mine to do: write. By the third class—I was still working on the same piece—I knew that if I had to continue my current jobs—making avocado-and-cheese sandwiches at a health food store and being a maid and dishwasher at a small inn—for the rest of my life so that I could write for a few hours a day, I would.

Ellen liked but did not love my writing. My first book got rejected by twenty-five publishers. Another writing teacher told me my writing was predictable and sentimental. It didn't stop me; I attended writing retreats, took writing workshops, enrolled in an MFA program as a nonmatriculating student, studied with mentors, copied sentences from Ernest Hemingway into my notebooks so that I could imitate his cadence. No one could convince me that what I felt, what I knew—that writing was how I knew what I didn't know I knew—should be ignored.

. . .

If I had a daughter, I would tell her this story so that she would feel free to trust what she knows. And I would say: Despite all that happened between my mother and me, she saved my life that day.

If I had a daughter, I would say:

If you notice that you feel darker and sadder when you think of perfecting the size of your body (or perfecting anything at all), know that you are focusing on a lie. When you feel lighter, happier, you know you are in the right place—the love of your heart. You are with the right people. You are doing what is right for you.

Fill yourself with what inspires you, not what you believe you have to do to be good or worthy or valuable. Even if it seems outlandish. If there is no mold for what you want to do, create one.

Be the only one.

Be the first.

Be yourself.

Know that sometimes you will feel as if you are thrashing and dissolving and everything around you is collapsing. It will pass. If you don't give it meaning, it will pass quickly. If you do give it meaning, it will also pass but not as quickly.

There's nothing out there, sweetheart. I know it looks like a big bad world sometimes. But when you change the lenses through which you are looking, what you see changes. The world becomes friendly.

You already know what is true. It's not in your head. It's not about understanding it or figuring it out. Decide what matters and then take back your attention from what doesn't.

You were born for this, my darling.

You can take it from here.

ACKNOWLEDGMENTS

During the four years I wrote this book, there were multiple times I felt as if I couldn't—why would anyone want to—dive back into some of the most painful moments of my life. Also there was (and still is) my very-much-alive mother, who reads every word I write, and would, I was certain, be one of the first people to read this—yet another book—with her as a main character. When I wanted to stop, write about anything else, or eat some chocolate, the following people walked me home. Without them, this book would not exist.

Celeste Fine
Whitney Frick
Rebecca Cole
Kim Rosen
Barbara Graham
Alice Josephs

Judy Ross
Lauren Matthews
The Dial Press team
My retreat students
Julie Plummer
Chris Abani
Kao Kalia Yang
Mike Magnuson
Anne Lamott
Luanne Lansing
Premsiri Lewin
Howard Roth
Our Tuesday sangha
and
Matt Weinstein,
of course and always

ABOUT THE AUTHOR

GENEEN ROTH is the author of eleven books, including the *New York Times* bestsellers *Women Food and God*, *When Food Is Love*, and *Lost and Found*. Her work has been translated into fourteen languages and has sold millions of copies worldwide. Over the past forty years, she has worked with thousands of women in workshops and retreats, deepening the themes that run through her books. Geneen has appeared on numerous national shows, including *The Oprah Winfrey Show*, *20/20*, *The Today Show*, *Good Morning America*, and *The View*. She lives in California and Hawaii.

ABOUT THE TYPE

This book was set in Fournier, a typeface named for Pierre-Simon Fournier (1712–68), the youngest son of a French printing family. He started out engraving woodblocks and large capitals, then moved on to fonts of type. In 1736 he began his own foundry and made several important contributions in the field of type design; he is said to have cut 147 alphabets of his own creation. Fournier is probably best remembered as the designer of St. Augustine Ordinaire, a face that served as the model for the Monotype Corporation's Fournier, which was released in 1925.